Dedication

GRANDFATHER'S BOOK
OLD-FASHIONED FUN FOR THE FAMILY

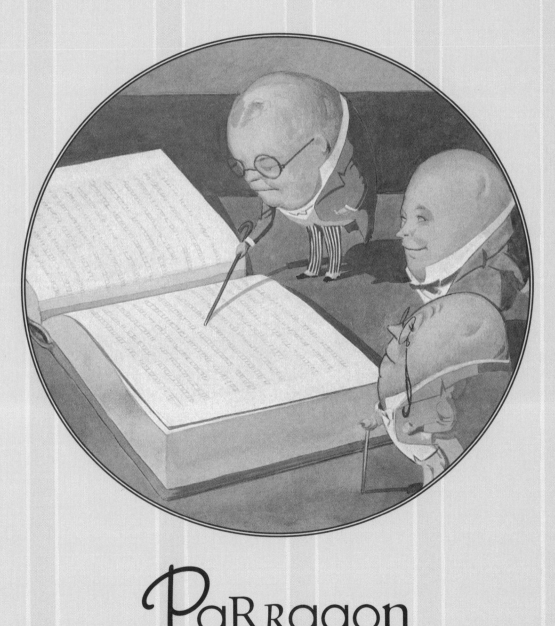

PaRragon

Bath New York Singapore Hong Kong Cologne Delhi Melbourne

This is a Parragon Publishing Book
This edition published in 2008

Parragon Publishing
Queen Street House
4 Queen Street
Bath BA1 1HE, UK

Designers: Timothy Shaner and Christopher Measom
Project Director: Alice Wong
Project Assistant: Deidra Garcia
Recipes and Activities Text by Monique Peterson
Line Illustrations for Activites by Sarah Kaplan

Printed in Thailand.
10 9 8 7 6 5 4 3 2 1

Contents

Contents

Contents

The person who has lived the most is not the one who has lived the longest, but the one with the richest experiences.

-Jean Jacques Rousseau

Two of Them

ANONYMOUS

Grandfather's come to see baby to-day,
Dear little, queer little baby Ned;
With his toothless mouth, his double chin,
And never a hair on his shiny head,
He looks in the pretty eyes of blue,
Where the baby's soul is peeping through,
And cries, with many a loving kiss,
'Hallo! what little old man is this?'

Baby stares in grandfather's face,
Merry old, cherry old 'Grandfather Ned,'
With his toothless mouth, his double chin,

And never a hair on his dear old head;
He scans him solemnly up and down,
From his double chin to his smooth, balk crown,
And says to himself as babies do,
'Hallo! can this be a baby, too?'

Grandfather Wisdoms

Genius is one percent inspiration and
ninety-nine percent perspiration.

—Thomas Edison

■

Experience is the mother of wisdom.
First think, and then speak.

■

Wise men talk because they have something to say;
fools, because they have to say something.

—Plato

■

It is not enough to have a good mind.
The main thing is to use it well.

—Rene Descartes

■

Ignorance is a cure for nothing.

—W.E.B. Du Bois

A man may die, nations may rise and fall, but an idea lives on. Ideas have endurance without death.

—JOHN F. KENNEDY

The most important part of the body is the brain.

—FRIDA KAHLO

Teachers open the door, but you must enter by yourself.

—CHINESE PROVERB

In a world that is changing all the time, no one's education is ever complete.

—MARGARET MEAD

13

Noisemakers

"*Children should be seen and not heard*" *is a time-honored saying. But sometimes it's fun to cut loose and make as much noise as possible along with your grandkids! You can make simple whistles and kazoos from perfectly ordinary items like paper, grass, combs, and toilet-paper rolls. Create a homemade orchestra and organize a whirlwind musical tour all around the house.*

WHISTLING GRASS

Find a wide, unbroken blade of grass about as long as your finger. Hold the blade of grass between your thumbs by pressing the flat sides of the grass with the sides of your thumbs. Your other fingers should be held in loose fists, and your thumbnails should be facing you. There should be a small gap, between the first and second joints on your thumbs, where you can see the blade of grass. Make sure the grass is stretched tightly across this gap. Put your lips to the hole and blow. You should make a high piercing whistle. If you're not getting a sound, try stretching the grass tighter or finding a broader blade.

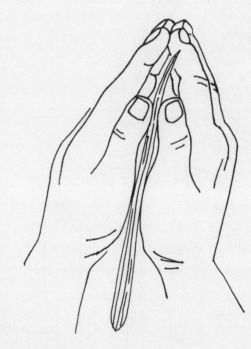

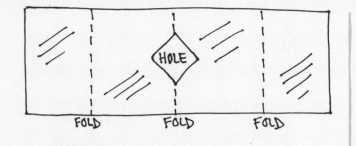

COMB WARBLER

Fold a piece of tissue paper over a medium-size hair comb. Place your lips against the comb and sing or hum to create a truly weird sound and tickling sensation.

KAZOO

Take a square of waxed paper and cover one end of an empty toilet paper roll. Secure the waxed paper with tape or a rubber band and make two slits in it. Hum through the open end of the tube to create a kazoo-like sound.

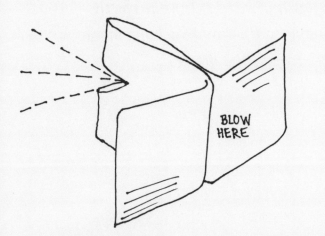

BLOW HERE

PAPER WHISTLE

Fold a piece of paper in half and cut a hole at the middle of the fold. Now, fold each side back so there is a crease facing you (*see above*). Hold your lips against the front crease and blow to produce an ear-splitting whistle!

The Frogs & The Well

Three frogs lived happily in a nice wet marsh. It got very hot one summer and the marsh dried up. The frogs had to look for a new home because frogs like nice damp places. They hopped and hopped around and soon came to a deep well. They took one great big leap to the side of the well and looked down. One frog said to the others, "This looks good. A nice dark well! Let us jump in!" But another, who was the wisest, said, "Wait just a minute! What if this well is dried up like the marsh? How will we get out if so? Let's keep searching."

Moral: Think before you act and look before you leap!

17

I come from Alabama with my banjo on my knee,
I'm goin' to Lou'siana, my true love for to see.

Oh! Susanna, Oh, don't you cry for me,
I've come from Alabama with my banjo on my knee.

It rained all night the day I left, the weather it was dry,
The sun so hot I froze to death! Susanna don't you cry.

Oh! Susanna, Oh, don't you cry for me,
I've come from Alabama with my banjo on my knee.

18

Oh! Susanna

LEGENDARY TALL TALES: PECOS BILL RIDES AGAIN

Pecos Bill was the greatest cowboy who ever lived. His adventures started way back when he was just a little critter. When Pecos was a baby, his family decided to pack up their wagon and head out West. Pecos had many brothers and sisters, so his mom and dad knew they'd have to find a place that was big enough to handle their family. Traveling on the wagon trail was rough, but Pecos didn't mind. At one stop they made, Pecos's mother put him down for a nap in the shade of a tree. Just then, a huge bear came stomping out of the woods. Pecos's family took one look, jumped back in their wagon, and high-tailed it out of there as fast as they could! Unfortunately, with all the kids around, they forgot about little Pecos, still asleep under that tree.

Pecos could have been in a lot of trouble, but luckily for him, a passing wolf noticed the little tyke and decided to adopt him. Pecos took to the wolf life immediately and grew up learning how to survive and have a wild time in the wilderness.

Pecos loved his wolf family, and probably would've stayed with them forever if a passing cowboy hadn't one day noticed him wrestling with his wolf brother.

"Howdy," said the cowboy.

"Howdy," answered Pecos.

"What's a young fella like yourself doing this far out in the wilderness all by his lonesome?"

"'Fella?'" said Pecos. "I'm not a fella. I'm a wolf."

"If you're a wolf, then where's your tail?" asked the cowboy.

Pecos looked down at his rear, but he

couldn't see a tail of any kind. He tried to catch sight of it and spun around and around faster and faster until he was dizzy.

The cowboy laughed. "Now, cut that out before you raise up a sandstorm. You are not a wolf—you're a boy. And if you are a boy, you might as well be a cowboy."

Pecos liked the sound of that. "But what kind of people are cowboys?" he asked.

"Well, we spend our days herding cattle across the open range. Most of us are reasonable folk, but there is one gang of cowboys that are as wild as a bunch of bucking broncos and as crazy as a pack of buzzards!"

This was the Fire Gulch Gang, and the more Pecos Bill heard about them, the more he knew he had to meet them.

After the cowboy had taught him all he knew about being a cowboy, Pecos said good-bye and set off to find the Fire Gulch Gang. It wasn't easy, since they always camped in the wildest, most dangerous parts of the land. Along the way he fought a giant rattlesnake and a fearsome mountain lion, who after that followed Pecos around like a couple of meek puppy dogs.

Finally, Pecos Bill came upon the Fire Gulch Gang. He marched into their camp and asked, "Who's the leader here?" The leader took one look at the snake around his neck and the ferocious mountain lion by his side and gulped. "I was, but you are now!" And that's how Pecos Bill became leader to the wildest, fiercest gang of cowpunchers the West had ever seen.

Pecos Bill and his gang had many amazing adventures together, and legends grew up around their exploits. A particular feat proved that no one and no *thing* on the planet could escape his lasso. One summer it was so hot that all the rivers and lakes on the prairie dried up. Everyone thought they'd have to move, because there wasn't enough water for the crops and the cattle. But, one day, the gang saw a dark thunder cloud on the horizon. They all cheered since this meant a nice, long thunderstorm would be coming and all the rivers and lakes would fill up again. But then everyone groaned when they saw that the storm was actually turning away from their camp.

"I guess we'll have to move after all," said one cowboy.

"Not if I can help it," Pecos Bill declared. He grabbed a lasso, jumped on his horse, and set off like lightning for the thunderstorm. Now, this wasn't any ordinary thunderstorm, but the biggest, wildest, wettest storm the West had ever seen. Pecos Bill rode up next to it, and then whirled his lasso over his head and hooked it onto the black cloud. Quick as a wink, Pecos was whisked up into the storm, and before he knew it, he was actually riding the wild cloud itself!

That storm almost threw Pecos Bill several times, but Pecos held on with all of his might, and eventually the storm stopped trying to fight so hard. Then, just like a man leading a horse, Pecos directed the storm over all the crops and cattle. The cowboys shouted with joy as the big, fat raindrops started pouring down on them, replenishing all the lakes and rivers. They could just make out Pecos, sitting on top of the black thundercloud, waving his hat and yelling for all he was worth!

Pecos loved his wild trip across the prairie. From then on, whenever life at the camp got a little too slow for him, he'd keep his eye out for a thunderstorm or two. As soon as he spotted one, he'd sneak off with his trusty lasso for another whirlwind ride! 🏃

Into the Woods

As every scouting grandfather knows, the secret to camping success is having good foresight. Pitching a perfect tent has less to do with the kind of tent you have and more to do with where you pitch it. By looking for potential troubles ahead of time, you can avoid them in the middle of the night. Similar principles apply to building campfires. With proper preparation, you can build one that will light right away, burn for hours, and last longer than the best ghost story ever told.

THE BEST TENT SPOT EVER

Even if your grandchildren aren't yet able to put up a tent by themselves, they can still do the most important part: picking and prepping the right spot. Here's how:

1. Choose a camping area away from stagnant pools of water, where mosquitoes may be breeding.

2. Scout the area for signs of animal activity, such as anthills, burrows, droppings, or tracks. Avoid pitching your tent on or near these, as you may receive unwanted visitors after the tent is up.

3. Survey the surface for a dry, flat, and even patch of bare ground.

4. Clear away pinecones, rocks, twigs, leaves, and similar loose ground cover.

5. Note the direction of the wind. If the tent door opens to the wind, unwanted rain and debris can blow easily into the tent.

6. Avoid pitching your tent in an open area or on top of a hill. These areas can be excessively windy and cause your tent to blow over.

7. Look out for low-hanging tree branches

that might drop sap, dew, pollen, or leaves on your tent.

8. Note which direction is east. You may not want the rising sun to shine directly in your window or door first thing in the morning.

THE FOUR-STEP ONE-MATCH CAMPFIRE

For best results, keep a long poker stick nearby and a bucket of water for emergency dousing.

1. **CLEAR** a circular area that will serve as your fire pit. If possible, arrange a ring of large stones around the circle to enclose the pit.

2. **GATHER** three types of materials: fine kindling, medium-size sticks, and large logs.

Kindling should be dry and brittle. Use such items as pinecones and needles, balled up newspaper, twigs, and leaves.

3. **STACK** a small pile of kindling in the fire pit. Arrange the sticks around the kindling in the shape of a tepee, with smaller pieces on the inside and larger pieces on the outside. Finally, lean three or four logs against the tepee. Be sure to leave room for air to circulate between the branches.

4. **LIGHT** the fire by striking a match and holding it at a downward angle to protect the flame from extinguishing. Light the kindling first by pushing the match through a space in the logs into the middle, then gently blow on the flames until they catch on the sticks. Then sit back, relax, and enjoy the flickering flames. Continue to add additional logs to the fire as the fire dies down.

Never leave a campfire unattended. When you're ready to turn in for the night, be sure to put out the fire completely with water. Then stir the ashes and douse with more water.

S.O.S. & Other Emergency Breakfasts

Grandfathers can lure even the sleepiest grandkids out of bed with the delicious smells of fried potatoes, eggs, or hotcakes. Even if the bread has gone stale, you can still make the best French toast. No time for pancakes? Just whip them up in the blender. Can't sit for a hot meal? Wrap it in a tortilla and make it instantly portable for a meal on the go. Try these family favorites with your grandchildren and shoo away the morning groggies in your household.

Rais'n Shine French Toast

3 eggs
4 tablespoons milk
1/4 teaspoon vanilla
1 tablespoon cinnamon
2 tablespoons sugar
Butter or oil for frying
8 slices raisin (or other) bread
Powdered sugar or maple syrup

1. Mix eggs, milk, vanilla, cinnamon, and sugar thoroughly in a shallow bowl.
2. Heat oil or butter in skillet or griddle on medium-high heat.
3. Dip each slice of bread in egg batter until covered, but do not soak.
4. Fry bread slices until brown crust forms on both sides.
5. Serve immediately, topped with butter and powdered sugar or maple syrup.

Makes four servings.

S.O.S. ("Stuff" on a Shingle)

$1/2$ pound lean ground beef
1 cup evaporated milk
2 tablespoons butter
Salt and pepper to taste
1 cup water
4 tablespoons flour
6 slices toast

1. Brown ground beef in hot frying pan until cooked through. Drain fat.
2. Stir in milk, butter, salt and pepper, and $1/2$ cup water. Bring to a simmer.
3. Meanwhile, mix remaining water with flour. Slowly stir into simmering beef. Remove from heat when mixture has thickened.
4. Spoon mixture over toast and serve hot.

Makes three servings.

Apple Hotcakes

1 egg
1 tablespoon sugar
1 tablespoon softened butter
1 apple, peeled, cored, and sliced
1 cup evaporated milk or buttermilk
1 cup pancake or biscuit mix
Oil or butter for frying
Maple syrup or apple butter

1. In blender, mix egg, sugar, butter, apple, and milk until smooth.
2. Add pancake or biscuit mix and blend.
3. Heat oil or butter in skillet or griddle over medium heat.
4. Drop batter by tablespoonfuls and fry until bubbles appear on top and edges become crisp. Flip once and heat through.
5. Serve warm with maple syrup or apple butter.

Makes four servings.

B'fast Burritos

1 tablespoon butter
1 potato, quartered and sliced
1/2 onion, chopped
4 beaten eggs
4 ounces turkey or other favorite pre-cooked sausage, sliced
4 ounces grated cheddar cheese
4 whole-wheat tortillas
Hot-pepper sauce to taste

1. Melt butter in frying pan over medium-high heat. Fry potatoes and onion, turning frequently, until brown and cooked through.
2. Stir in beaten eggs and turkey sausage. Heat until eggs are at desirable consistency.
3. Sprinkle grated cheese on top and allow it to melt.
4. Place a serving of scrambled mixture in the center of each tortilla. Add pepper sauce to taste, and then wrap with tortilla and serve.
5. If you're making these to go, wrap each burrito in aluminum foil to keep warm.

Makes four servings.

29

Caterpillar

BY CHRISTINA ROSSETTI

Brown and furry
Caterpillar in a hurry,
Take your walk
To the shady leaf, or stalk,
Or what not,
Which may be the chosen spot.
No toad spy you,
Hovering bird of prey pass by you;
Spin and die,
To live again a butterfly.

The Fly & The Moth

One night, a fly noticed an open jar of strawberry jam on a table. The jam looked so sweet and tasty that he immediately flew inside the jar to have a treat. Unfortunately, he became stuck in the sticky jam. As he was struggling to get out, a moth flew by and instead of helping him said, "It serves you right! Didn't you realize how thick and sticky that jam would be before you jumped into it?" A little while later, someone turned a lamp on in the room, and the moth, who could not resist the light, smacked into it again and again until he had a big headache. "What's this?" said the fly, who had managed to scramble out of the jar finally. "You scolded me for my sweet tooth, but you yourself are playing with fire!"

Moral: Do not criticize your friends' mistakes and ignore your own.

Reading the Clouds

*C*louds are more than streaks of puffy whiteness that decorate the sky. These massive formations of water vapor bring rain and snow as well as protection from the sun's hot rays. By learning how to recognize different clouds and their formations, you and your grandchildren can practice age-old ways of predicting the weather and staying in touch with nature.

CUMULUS

These puffy cotton-candy clouds are commonly seen against a clear blue summer backdrop of sky. They're a sign of fair weather and are perfect for viewing while lying on your back on a grassy knoll. As they drift lazily across the sky, see what shapes and characters they conjure up for you and your grandchild.

CIRRUS

You'll see thin, wispy, curly cirrus clouds higher in the sky than other clouds, anywhere from three to ten miles overhead. These clouds are made up almost entirely of ice crystals and often signal that a storm is on its way within 18 to 36 hours.

CIRROSTRATUS

High-altitude cirrostratus clouds form large, wispy sheets across the sky. They often look like large zebra stripes, which is a sure indication of bad weather to come. These clouds often loom above thunderheads, so be sure to seek cover if you see them.

STRATUS

The word *stratus* comes from the word stratum, which means layer. This is the name for the flat, thick clouds that hover near the ground. These clouds are mostly made of water droplets but they don't produce rain. If you're stuck in the middle of a stratus cloud, expect to be misted by drizzle.

Red Sky at Night, Sailor's Delight;
Red Sky at Morning, Sailor Take Warning
In mid-latitude regions, weather patterns tend to move from west to east. A reddish morning sky indicates that the sun is shining on banks of clouds approaching from the west. In the evening, a red sky can indicate that the sun is shining on eastern cloud formations that have already moved through the area.

NIMBOSTRATUS

These low-hanging, flat clouds are often shapeless but easy to identify because they are darker in color than other clouds. *Nimbus* is the Roman word for "rain cloud"—so named because the bottoms of these clouds are heavy with falling raindrops or snow.

FOG

The difference between fog and low-lying stratus clouds is that fog touches the surface of the earth. Fog appears when a cold front has moved into an area with warmer air. When the cold and warm air meet, the naturally occurring water vapor in the air condenses into a thick mist. Although fog isn't necessarily an indicator of bad weather, its blinding whiteness can pose a hazard.

A Ring Around the Moon
Means a Storm Is Coming Soon
Moon rings are caused by light refracted by the ice crystals in cirrus and cirrostratus clouds. This bright halo around the moon is usually an indicator of an approaching cold front. The brighter the ring, the nearer the storm.

A Fairy Tale Verse

Miss Goldilocks, out walking, spied
The Three Bears' house and went inside.
She sipped some supper from each cup,
And ate the wee bear's porridge up.
Three easy chairs she found to try,
But one was hard and one too high;
'Twas baby bear's she liked the best.
Then wishing for a bit of rest

Goldilocks

She sampled all the beds upstairs
And went to sleep in a baby bear's.
But when she woke, and by the bed
Saw all the bears, she quickly fled.

38

Kitchen-Sink Pizzas

Announce "Pizza!" and you have a surefire way to get even the pickiest of picky eaters excited about lunch or dinner. You can make pizza out of just about anything in the pantry or refrigerator, including leftovers! Use English muffins, focaccia, frozen crescent rolls, pita bread—you can even make pizza sandwiches. Even when the cupboard is bare, you can usually drum up a little marinara sauce and shredded cheese, and you've got pizza. Try variations on some of these nontraditional recipes, and taste the goodness of your own Kitchen-Sink Pizzas.

Crunchy Crescent Pizzas

1 (8-ounce) can crescent rolls
6 ounces cream cheese
Assorted sliced or chopped raw veggies
(broccoli, cucumber, cauliflower,
zucchini, squash, peppers, alfalfa
sprouts, snap peas, carrots)
Assorted sliced or chopped raw fruit
(melon, strawberries, kiwi, banana,
apple, grapes, blueberries, mango)

1. Preheat oven to 400°F.
2. Roll out crescent dough pieces evenly into one single sheet on a 10- by 15-inch baking sheet. Press dough with fingertips to eliminate seams between the segments. Prick dough with fork in several places.
3. Bake for 10 minutes or until golden. Cool on wire rack.
4. Spread cream cheese evenly over crust.
5. Let your grandchildren make faces or funny patterns with the fruit and vegetable toppings.
6. Slice into squares, and serve cold.

Makes six to eight servings

Mediterranean Pita Pizzas

4 whole-wheat pitas
8 tablespoons tapenade (a spread
made with black olives, capers,
and anchovies)
1 medium-size red onion, sliced
1 large tomato, sliced
8 ounces feta cheese
Dried basil
Dried oregano

1. Preheat oven to 375°F.
2. Cut through each pita to make 2 rounds. Arrange pita halves on nonstick baking sheet.
3. Spread 1 tablespoon tapenade on each pita round. Layer each round with equal amounts of onion, tomato, and cheese. Sprinkle tops with dried basil and oregano to taste.
4. Bake for 10 minutes.

Makes four servings.

Spud Pizzas

4 baking potatoes
2 tomatoes, sliced
10 ounces mozzarella cheese, sliced
4 slices Canadian bacon, cut in strips
Italian seasoning to taste
Olive oil for drizzling
Salt and pepper to taste

1. Preheat broiler.
2. Scrub potatoes and prick several times with a fork.
3. Cook potatoes in microwave on high for 10 to 12 minutes until done, rotating halfway through.
4. Cut three slits into each potato and stuff each slit with tomato, cheese, and bacon.
5. Sprinkle a dash of Italian seasoning into each slit, then drizzle olive oil on tops of potatoes. Add salt and pepper to taste.
6. Broil spud pizzas for about 5 minutes, or until cheese is melted.

Makes four servings.

Leftover-Lovers' Pizza

1 large prepared pizza crust
1 cup leftover spaghetti sauce
(homemade or ready-made)
$1/2$ cup left-over cooked hamburger,
soyburger, or shredded chicken
or turkey
$1/2$ cup salad greens or spinach (fresh
or thawed and dried)
1 cup shredded mozzarella cheese
2 tablespoons olive oil
Cornmeal

1. Preheat oven to 400°F.
2. Spread sauce evenly on top of prepared pizza crust.
3. Top with meat, greens, and cheese.
4. Drizzle olive oil on top.
5. Sprinkle a small handful of corn-meal on a pizza stone or baking sheet and place pizza on top.
6. Bake for 20 minutes or until crust is brown and cheese is melted.

Makes two or three servings.

I would be true, for there are
those who trust me,

I would be pure, for there are
those who care,

I would be strong, for there
is much to suffer,

I would be brave, for there is
much to dare,

I would be a friend of all, the
foe, the friendless,

I would be giving and forget
the gift,

I would be humble, for I
know my weakness,

I would look up, and laugh
and love and live.

—ANONYMOUS

LEGENDARY TALL TALES: HOW DAVY CROCKETT BECAME A CONGRESSMAN

many, many stories are told about the great frontiersman and hunter, Davy Crockett—most told by the man himself! Davy boasted that he was half-horse, half-alligator, with just a touch of snapping turtle. Legends say that he single-handedly tamed a panther and that he caused a raccoon to fall out of a tree just by outsmiling it.

Davy Crockett seemed bigger than life. And although he is well known for his outdoor adventures, did you know that he was also a congressman? It's hard to believe this rough-and-tumble man was a representative in Washington, D.C., but he was. He supported Native-American rights to land and wanted farmers to have more say in the government. But Davy Crockett had to fight to become a congressman too, and here is one legend of how he did it.

One day, Davy traveled to a town to give a speech and gather votes for himself. He showed up late (on account of a cougar he had to battle along the way!) and found that his opponent was already giving a very long speech.

"Now no one's going to listen to what I have to say," thought Davy. And it was true—once his opponent's long, boring speech was over, people began to drift away. Until Davy Crockett got up and declared that the debates should be moved to the local restaurant and saloon, where meals and drinks would be on him! Everyone cheered and charged into the establishment. Soon, everyone was having a grand old time, eating and drinking, all thanks to Mr. Davy Crockett!

But when the bill showed up, Davy

was amazed to see how much everything cost. He told Brown, the owner, "I wasn't quite expecting such a large crowd to turn out. Why don't you keep this on record and I'll come back tomorrow and pay you everything I owe?"

Brown told Davy he'd have to pay; otherwise he would throw Davy in jail. Davy thought he'd be in big trouble, but then he remembered an old bearskin he had with him and decided to offer it up as payment. He gave it to Brown, and the bill was settled.

So Davy again went to the center of the village and began making a speech. But it had taken him so long to settle the matter of the bill that everyone was bored and hungry again. They called for another meal, and Davy of course obliged, amid many cheers of "Hurray for Davy Crockett!"

This time, Davy *knew* the owner would not be happy with him. And to make matters worse, he had no more bearskins to trade. He was just about to give up and head over to the jail, when he saw that Brown had folded the bearskin up and left it carelessly hanging off the end of the counter. Quick as a wink, Davy snatched it up. He did it so fast that no one noticed him take it.

"I hope you won't mind another bearskin as payment?" he asked Brown, as he handed over the bearskin again.

Davy could not believe it. And what was even more unbelievable was that the trick worked two more times! Each time the group would crowd into the restaurant and eat and drink to their hearts' delight, then Davy would pinch the bearskin and pay again. He paid for four different meals with the same skin. And he knew the people who had heard him that day would be sure to vote for him. And so, with a little help from a bearskin, Davy Crockett became a congressman. 🏃

Don't Lose Your Beans!

There are no age limits required for Mancala (considered the world's oldest game) which is why old and young alike can enjoy playing together. Each player tries to figure out how—by moving beans around the game board—to end up with more beans in their store than their opponent. Introduce your grandchildren to a basic version of this generational favorite by constructing the playing board and then testing your strategy against one another time and time again.

Bottom of an empty dozen-egg carton, two cups, 36 dried beans (or pebbles or marbles)

1. Position the egg carton between the two players with the long sides facing them. Place a cup at each end of the carton.

2. Place three beans in each of the egg carton depressions, or "pots." Leave the end cups, or "stores," empty. Each player claims the cup to the right as their "store," and owns the row of six "pots" in front of them.

3. Flip a coin to determine who goes first.

4. The first player removes all the beans from one of their pots. Then, starting with the pot to the left of the one emptied, the player drops, or "sows," one bean in each adjacent consecutive pot—including both stores and the opponent's pots—in a counterclockwise direction around the board. If the last bean lands in their own store, the player takes another turn. Otherwise, the play passes to the other player.

5. The game continues with each player taking turns sowing beans around the board.

The game ends when one player has no more beans in their pots. The player with the most beans in their store wins.

GAME VARIATION:

1. Flip a coin to determine who goes first.

2. Players take turns sowing beans in each pot counterclockwise around the board, including their own store but skipping their opponent's store. If the last bean a player sows lands in their own store, the player gets another turn. If the last bean a player sows ends up in an empty pot on their side, then that player captures all the beans from the opponent's pot directly opposite and puts them in their store.

3. The game continues until one player has cleared all the beans from the pots on their side of the board. If, in the next turn, the opponent can sow beans onto the empty side of the board, the play continues. If not, the remaining beans go into the player's store. The player with the most beans in their store wins.

The Field of Corn

An old man had a field, and when he became very ill he sent for his three sons to tell them how to divide it up when he died. "My boys," the old man said, "there's one thing that I want you to do. I have left a rich gift for all of you, but you'll have to search for it in the field." Before they could ask any questions, the old man passed away. The three sons were heartbroken, and didn't even think of the gift their father had left them for many days. But eventually, thoughts of treasure and gold seeped into their minds and they decided to dig up the field to look for the gift. They worked hard and dug up all the soil, but didn't find anything. "That's so weird," one son said. "Why would Dad tell us there was something in this field? We haven't found a single coin or jewel." His brother sighed. "Well, we've already dug the field up. We might as well plant some corn here and make the most of it." So the brothers planted, and the next season, they had a field of beautiful, rich, golden corn, ten times bigger than any crop that had grown when their father planted. Suddenly, each of the sons realized that the gift their father had wanted to give them wasn't riches or jewels, but the joy of seeing their hard work pay off.

Moral: Search until you find, and your hard work will be rewarded.

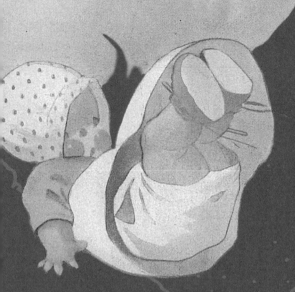

Twenty Little Raindrops

by Mildred Plew Merryman

Twenty little raindrops, laughing out aloud,
Tightly tied their bonnets on and tumbled from a cloud.
Two darted downward to dance from place to place,
Two bounced upon a roof, two ran a race;
But one was very dizzy
From his recent trip so whizzy,
So he met a little bird and washed its face.

Two little raindrops trickled through the trees,
Two preferred excitement so they coasted on the breeze,
Two little raindrops softly sat them down
Plump on the point of a steeple in the town;
But one was very merry
So he lighted on a fairy
And there he sat, a twinkle in her crown.

Twenty little raindrops, laughing out aloud,
Tightly tied their bonnets on and tumbled from a cloud.
Two made a rainbow with a sunset beam,
Three that were daring dove into a running stream,
But one was very lazy
So he crawled into a daisy
And dreamed a little raindrop dream.

He that is good at making excuses
is seldom good at anything else.

—BENJAMIN FRANKLIN

Happiness comes when your work
and your words are of benefit to
yourself and to others.

—BUDDHA

It takes less time to do a thing right
than to explain why you did it wrong.

—HENRY WADSWORTH LONGFELLOW

Laziness may appear attractive,
but work gives satisfaction.

—ANNE FRANK

If you want a job done right, do it yourself.

■

Don't bite off more than you can chew.

■

Never leave that till tomorrow which
you can do today.

—BENJAMIN FRANKLIN

■

When you are asked if you can
do a job, tell 'em, "Certainly
I can." Then get busy and
find out how to do it.

—TEDDY ROOSEVELT

■

Where there's a
will there's a way.

—GEORGE HERBERT

EZ Soups & Salads

No matter how many grandchildren you have, it pays to master the art of making quick, great-tasting meals using simple, accessible ingredients. Keep the refrigerator stocked with bags of prewashed salad blends as well as lunch meats, cheese, and fruit. Then, when the grandkids pop by for a visit, it's always a cinch to toss together an easy lunch or dinner for everyone.

Split Pea & Sausage Soup

1 (16-ounce) package dried split peas
4 ounces smoked sausage links,
sliced and quartered
7 cups water
1 onion, chopped
2 carrots, chopped
1 teaspoon salt
1 teaspoon Italian seasoning
1/2 teaspoon pepper
Croutons
Parmesan cheese

1. Rinse peas with cold water in colander.
2. Place all ingredients (except croutons and cheese) in 5-quart Dutch oven. Bring to a boil over high heat.
3. Reduce heat and simmer uncovered for about an hour or until peas are tender, stirring occasionally.
4. Remove sausage with slotted spoon and set aside.
5. In 3-cup batches, puree soup with blender or food processor.
6. Return soup and sausage to Dutch oven and reheat over medium flame.
7. Ladle soup into bowls and top with croutons and Parmesan cheese. Serve immediately.

Makes six servings.

Farmhouse Soup

2 pounds green beans, cut in thirds
2 large potatoes, scrubbed and diced
Water
1 cup bacon, diced
1 onion, chopped
Salt and pepper to taste

1. Place beans and potatoes in soup pot and add water until vegetables are just covered. Cook over high heat until simmering, then lower to medium heat.

2. While soup is heating, sauté bacon and onions in large skillet, about 5 minutes or until onions are soft.
3. Add bacon and onion mixture to soup pot and continue cooking soup until potatoes are tender. (Add more water if necessary for desired consistency.)
4. Add salt and pepper to taste. Serve immediately.

Makes four servings.

Quick-Fix Salad Dressing

3 tablespoons olive oil
1 tablespoon vinegar
1 teaspoon mustard
2 teaspoons mayonnaise
1 teaspoon honey
Salt and pepper to taste

Whisk all ingredients together until blended.

Makes four servings.

Simple Caesar–y Salad

2 potatoes, peeled and sliced coarsely
1 package Caesar salad mix
with dressing
2 hard-boiled eggs, quartered,
Anchovies (optional)

1. Place the potato slices in a soup pot with water to cover. Boil until tender but not mushy. Allow to cool.
2. In a large bowl, toss the Caesar salad with the dressing and the potatoes.
3. Garnish with egg quarters and, for adventurous grandchildren, anchovies.

Makes four servings.

Peachy Luncheon Salad

1 bag prewashed romaine lettuce
8 slices turkey or ham, cut in thin strips
$1/2$ cup shredded cheese
2 peaches, sliced
Your favorite salad dressing
(or Quick-Fix Salad Dressing)

1. Divide the romaine lettuce among 4 bowls.
2. Top each with even amounts of meat, cheese, and peach slices.
3. Drizzle with salad dressing and serve.

Makes four servings.

Did you ever?

Did you ever see a match box,
or a garden fence?

Psychic Parlor Amusements

It's always good to have some parlor tricks up your sleeve for instant entertainment and a few laughs. Try these tricks on your grandchildren before teaching them the secrets. Then the next time you want to amuse friends and family members, offer to play the role of assistant and watch your grandchildren have fun showing off their special "extrasensory" abilities.

TRICKY DICE
Large clear glass of water, three acrylic dice

Start by asking a volunteer to drop three dice into the water. Ask them to hold the glass above their head and, without letting anyone else sneak a peek, look at the numbers on the bottoms of the dice and add them together in their head. When your volunteer places the glass back on the table, dip your finger into the water and touch your forehead. Close your eyes and concentrate deeply, then announce the total. Watch your volunteer's face light up when you say the right answer.

THE SECRET: When you dip your finger into the water, take a quick glance at the tops of the dice. Add the totals in your head while you're "concentrating," then subtract that number from 21. (The tops and bottoms of dice always total seven, so you can do this trick with as many dice as you want; simply multiply the number of dice you use by seven to know the number you need to subtract the total from.)

MIND-READING MAGIC DECK OF CARDS

This trick works best when you have a ready audience of friends or family members. Ask for a volunteer from the group to stand and face the others while holding a deck of cards facedown behind their back. Blindfold your volunteer and ask them to pick a card from the middle of the deck, and then have them hold the card with its face touching their forehead and its back facing the audience. At this time, instruct your audience to focus on the drawn card and concentrate deeply until a particular image comes to mind. Tell them that in a group, the powers of ESP can be very strong, and the chances of being able to "read" the mystery card can be greatly improved. Then, ask your volunteer to slip the drawn card into his back pocket.

Take back the remaining deck of cards and remove the blindfold. Ask your volunteer to pick anyone in the audience to guess the mystery card. That person names the card, and when the volunteer pulls the card out of his back pocket, it is the very same card the audience member named.

THE SECRET: Before you begin the trick, flip the top and bottom cards of the deck. Your volunteer will think they are holding the deck upside down. When the volunteer pulls a card from the pack and touches it to their forehead, they'll think the back of the card is facing the audience—but in reality, they're revealing the face of the card to the entire crowd.

A Fairy Tale Verse

Jack's the widow's boy who sold
Her cow for beans instead of gold;
The beans grew up to very high
That Jack one day climbed to the sky
And found the wicked giant's lair
(With only Mrs. Giant there);
He took the magic hen away
And called again the second day.

Jack and the Beanstalk

But on the third, the giant grim
In rage descended after him,
Jack quickly chopped the beanstalk down
And thus the giant broke his crown!

66

Legendary Tall Tales: The Mission of Johnny Appleseed

here are plenty of stories about tough cowboys, cunning pioneers, and steely lawmen in America. But one of the most famous legends is about a man who wasn't strong or violent or rough. In fact, this man became known far and wide because he was the complete opposite. He was kind and peaceful, and he only wanted to live in harmony with nature and help his fellow men. His name was Johnny Appleseed, and it's because of him that thousands of apple trees grew and prospered in the middle of America.

Many stories are told about Johnny Appleseed. He roamed by himself from New York all the way to Michigan, Ohio, and Illinois. He never bothered to build a house or buy things, and he lived a very peaceful life, traveling through the land.

The American wilderness was a very dangerous place in the late 18th century, before many towns were built, but Johnny didn't carry a knife or a gun, and Native-American tribes didn't attack him. They respected him and let him pass on his way since he never caused trouble and respected the land. Wild animals never frightened him, and once during a fierce blizzard he crawled into an abandoned tree trunk only to encounter a mother bear and her two cubs hibernating inside! Instead of running for the hills, Johnny simply curled up next to them and had a good night's sleep, completely at ease with the enormous creatures beside him.

He did small odd jobs for settlers he met, and only requested some food or old clothing as payment. This sometimes made him look pretty funny, since the clothes often didn't fit, and he usually didn't own shoes and wore a steel pot for a hat! He didn't see the need for fancy clothes or transportation, and instead spent his days traveling on foot or by canoe, living as one with nature and the creatures of the land.

Johnny Appleseed's love and respect for nature included all animals, no matter how fierce or dangerous they were. One day, he came upon a wolf caught in a hunter's trap. The wolf snarled and lunged at Johnny when he approached, but it was obvious the animal was in a lot of pain and pretty exhausted.

"There, there," Johnny said in a low, comforting voice. Bit by bit he made his way toward the wounded animal, and miraculously, the wolf grew calm. Carefully, Johnny pried open the trap and studied the wolf's leg. He was pretty badly hurt, so Johnny gathered medicinal herbs and tore a long bandage from his tattered shirt. He took care of the wolf until the wound healed.

In fact, Johnny took such good care of him that the wolf began following him around like a faithful puppy dog. Johnny finally had to send him back to his den though, as the sight of a ferocious wolf calmly walking by his side had a tendency to scare the willies out of people!

Because Johnny loved his animal friends so much, it often made him sad when he saw people hunting them. He himself only ate vegetables, berries, and grains, but he understood that people needed to have food. Otherwise they would starve. The Midwest was a tough place, and sometimes it was very difficult to plant crops or maintain a farm. People were often hungry and had to rely on what they caught to survive.

"If only there was a way to bring food to the people without having them hunt animals every day or go hungry," Johnny thought as he rested beneath a glorious apple tree, full of beautiful white blossoms. Suddenly he jumped up. "Why, the answer's right in front of my face! I'll collect apple seeds and plant them across this whole great nation. When the apples ripen, everyone will have something to eat. No one will have to go hungry again!" And he began collecting the seeds immediately.

Johnny traveled across several states, planting apple seeds and giving away small trees to settlers as he went. Instead of simply providing people with food once, he gave them the gift of apples, which would grow again and again. Settlers were always eager to see Johnny Appleseed, as they knew that soon enough their kitchens would be full of delicious, juicy apples.

Because of his peaceful ways and kindness, Johnny Appleseed left a permanent mark on America. Even today you can visit the Midwest and view the beautiful apple trees Johnny planted to help make the world a more gentle and loving place. 🏃

Old-Time Quenchers

*O*n a hot summer day, old-fashioned coolers never go out of style. Nothing tastes quite as good as fresh-squeezed lemonade from the fruit of the back-yard tree, or ginger ale made with freshly chopped ginger. Share these generational thirst quenchers with your grandchildren and let them have fun "juicing up" at a neighborhood barbecue or roadside lemonade stand (see page 176).

Roadside Lemonade

1½ cups sugar
6 cups water
1½ cups fresh-squeezed lemon juice
(about 8 to 10 lemons)
Ice cubes

1. Mix sugar and 2 cups water in large saucepan and bring to a boil.
2. Reduce heat and simmer, stirring occasionally, until sugar dissolves.
4. Remove from heat and cool.
5. Stir juice into syrup.
6. Stir the above mixture into remaining water in 2½-quart container. Refrigerate until cold.
7. Serve in tall glasses over ice cubes.

Makes about two quarts.

LIMEADE: Substitute limes for lemons.

ORANGEADE: Decrease lemon juice to 1 cup. Substitute 4 cups fresh-squeezed orange juice for the 4 cups of water in step 6.

GRAPEFRUITADE: Decrease lemon juice to ½ cup. Substitute 4 cups fresh-squeezed grapefruit juice for the water in step 6.

Homemade Root Beer

1 teaspoon dry yeast
$1/2$ cup warm water
2 cups sugar
1 quart hot water
1-gallon jar
4 teaspoons root-beer extract

1. In small bowl, dissolve yeast in warm water.
2. In large bowl, dissolve sugar in hot water.
3. In gallon jar, mix contents of both bowls and root-beer extract.
4. Fill jar with warm water, stir, and cover.
5. Set jar in warm, sunny spot for 4 hours. Keep root beer covered until the following day, when it will be ready to drink.
6. Chill root beer before serving.

Makes ten to twelve servings.

Fresh Ginger Ale

*2 cups fresh ginger, peeled
and chopped
3 strips lemon peel
4 cups water
1 1/2 cups sugar
3 quarts chilled seltzer or club soda
Ice cubes*

1. Place ginger, lemon peel, and water in large saucepan. Bring to a boil and simmer uncovered for about 10 minutes.
2. Stir in sugar and boil for another 15 minutes or so, until the liquid is reduced to about 3 cups.
3. Pour syrup through a sieve and discard ginger and lemon peel.
4. Allow syrup to cool, then cover and chill for at least two hours.
5. To serve, fill tall glasses with ice cubes, pour about 1/4 cup syrup into each glass, and add 1 cup seltzer or club soda. Stir and sip!

Makes about twelve servings.

Cherry-Lime Rickey

*Ice cubes
1 lime, quartered
8 ounces soda water
2 tablespoons cherry syrup
Maraschino cherries,
chopped (optional)*

1. Fill a tall glass with ice and squeeze juice from lime wedges into it.
2. Pour soda water over the ice, add the cherry syrup, and stir. For extra flavor, mix the chopped cherries into the rickey.

VARIATIONS: Substitute lemon or orange for the lime; add strawberry or raspberry syrup instead of cherry.

Makes one serving.

ACTIVITIES

Birds of a Feather

Spending time observing nature is a wonderful way to share discoveries with your grandchildren. Bird-watching is more than simply looking for and identifying birds: It's learning how to listen for specific songs, calls, and other noises, such as tapping or drumming. Plan your excursion and take along binoculars, a tape recorder, and a sketch pad to take descriptive notes or draw pictures of the birds you see.

Most bird-watchers learn to identify birds by their vocalizations, which tend to be specific to a species; however, some birds mimic other sounds. Catbirds, or mockingbirds, for example, copy the songs of other songbirds, and starlings will mimic car alarms and even human voices!

Here are some sounds to listen for:
- Certain water birds, such as geese, ducks, and swans, are identifiable by honks, quacks, and hoots.
- Sparrows and warblers repeat the same note quickly so that it sounds like a trill, a twitter, or a churr.

- Woodpeckers make rhythmical tapping or drumming sounds while looking for insects in tree bark.
- Grouse and prairie chickens make drumming and booming noises to attract mates.

Whether on a walk in the country, a nature preserve, or through an urban neighborhood, be on the lookout for abandoned or empty nests such as these:

- Along rocky beaches and shellbars, look for shallow, scratched-out depressions in the ground or leaves, called **SCRAPES**. Such nests are common among certain coastal birds, such as the red-billed black or American oystercatcher.

- Look for elevated **PLATFORM** nests in treetops or in areas of shallow water. Hawks, cormorants, eagles, herons, and ospreys build these flat, slightly depressed nests to keep their eggs out of the reach of predators.
- Most songbirds build **CUPPED** nests, which are round and solidly built. These are complex bird nests designed to keep eggs warm and protected.
- **ADHERENT** nests are plastered under the eves of buildings, along stone ledges, or barn walls. If you spot such a cup-shaped nest built of mud, chances are you're looking at the home of a barn swallow.
- Vireos build **PENSILE** nests, cup-shaped structures that hang from tree branches by their stiffly woven rims.
- If you see a cup-shaped nest that looks like a small bag swinging freely from a tree branch, you've probably found a **PENDULOUS** nest built by an oriole.

...Flock Together

You may know that a group of birds is called a **FLOCK**, but did you know that a group of chickens is called a **PEEP**, or that a group of hummingbirds is called a **TROUBLING**? Here are words for some other flocks:

A **FLIGHT** of cormorants ■ A **MURDER** of crows ■ A **DULE** of doves ■ A **PADDLING** of ducks ■ A **CONVOCATION** of eagles ■ A **CHARM** of finches ■ A **GAGGLE** of geese ■ A **COLONY** of gulls ■ A **BROOD** of hens ■ A **BAND** of jays ■ A **CONCENTRATION** of kingfishers ■ An **EXALTATION** of larks ■ A **RAFT** of loons ■ A **TIDING** of magpies ■ A **WISDOM** of owls ■ A **COMPANY** of parrots ■ A **COVEY** of quail ■ A **CONSPIRACY** of ravens ■ A **PARLIAMENT** of rooks ■ A **QUARREL** of sparrows ■ A **MURMURATION** of starlings ■ A **BALLET** of swans

It Can Be Done

ANONYMOUS

The man who misses all the fun
Is he who says, "It can't be done."
In solemn pride he stands aloof
And greets each venture with reproof.
Had he the power he'd efface
The history of the human race;
We'd have no radio or motor cars,
No streets lit by electric stars;
No telegraph nor telephone,
We'd linger in the age of stone.
The world would sleep if things were run
By men who say, "It can't be done."

The Goose with the Golden Eggs

Once upon a time, an old farmer and his wife discovered they had a goose that laid one beautiful egg made of solid gold each morning. At first they were overjoyed, but then they thought that it was pretty slow work for the goose to lay only one egg a day. They thought all the eggs must be stored inside the goose, so they cut her up to get the eggs. To their dismay, they didn't find any golden eggs, and the goose was just like any other goose. Instead of having one golden egg a day, they now had no eggs at all.

Moral: Those who always want more often end up with nothing at all.

What happens when ~ ~

I burst into tears

or when ~ I am frozen with a glance ~

82

83

A Fairy Tale Verse

Quaint Alice trailed the rabbit, dressed
So strangely in a coat and vest
And at the bottom of the hole,
Had many more adventures droll;
By tasting "Drink Me" she grew smaller,
By sipping something else, was taller;
She met the Duchess, Cheshire Cat,
The Mad March Hare and folk like that,

Alice in Wonderland

She stirred her tea and played croquet,
In court had nothing right to say,
And when it all began to seem
Mixed up, discovered 'twas a dream.

Savory Snacks

Nothing beats homemade snacks after school, after a soccer game, or during a movie on a rainy day. The treat can begin in the kitchen with simple and quick recipes that make it easy to introduce young grandchildren to cooking. Start by looking in your freezer, refrigerator, or pantry for ingredients you probably already have. From start to finish, these finger-licking snacks can be ready to eat in less than a half hour. Yum!

Down-home Potato Chips

2 medium-size red potatoes, scrubbed
2 tablespoons herbs or spices (such as dill, rosemary, dried onion flakes, or BBQ seasoning)
1/2 teaspoon garlic salt
1/4 teaspoon pepper
Nonstick cooking spray
1 tablespoon olive oil

1. Preheat oven to 450°F.
2. Slice potatoes very thin and pat dry with paper towels.
3. In small bowl, combine herbs, garlic salt, and pepper. Set aside.
4. Coat baking sheet with nonstick cooking spray and arrange potato slices in a single layer on the sheet.
5. Spray potato slices with cooking spray and bake 10 minutes.
6. Turn slices over and brush with oil. Sprinkle herb mixture evenly onto slices. Bake for 5 to 10 minutes longer, or until chips are golden brown.
7. Cool on baking sheet before serving.

Makes four to six servings.

Bruschetta Bites

2 cloves garlic, minced
3 plum tomatoes, diced
3/4 cup olive oil
10 to 15 fresh basil leaves,
finely chopped
Salt and pepper to taste
1 baguette, cut in 1/2-inch slices

1. In medium-size bowl, mix together garlic, tomatoes, oil, and basil. Stir in salt and pepper to taste. Set aside.
2. Heat 1 to 2 tablespoons olive oil in large skillet over medium heat. Grill baguette slices on both sides.
3. Top bread slices with tomato mixture and serve immediately.

Makes four to six servings.

Dogs in Blankets

8 hot dogs (veggie, beef, pork,
chicken, or turkey)
8 thin slices cheese
1 (8-ounce) package crescent rolls
Mustard

1. Preheat oven to 375°F.
2. Cut a partial slit lengthwise
   down the middle of each hot dog
   and fill it with a slice of cheese.
3. Wrap each hot dog with a seg-
   ment of crescent-roll dough.
4. Place hot dogs on a baking sheet
   and bake for about 12 minutes,
   or until rolls are golden brown.
5. Cut hot dogs into thirds and
   serve hot with mustard.

Makes twenty-four servings.

Cheesy Chicken Nuggets

$1/2$ cup bread crumbs
$1/4$ teaspoon pepper
$1/4$ cup finely grated cheddar cheese

1 teaspoon dried basil
$1/2$ teaspoon salt
4 boneless chicken breasts,
cut into bite-size pieces
$1/2$ cup melted butter
Barbecue sauce (or honey mustard
sauce or ranch dressing)

1. Preheat oven to 400°F.
2. In large bowl, combine bread
   crumbs, pepper, cheddar cheese,
   basil, and salt, and mix until
   well blended.
3. Dip each chicken piece in the
   melted butter, then roll in the
   crumb mixture until coated.
4. Place nuggets on nonstick baking
   sheet and bake for 10 to 15 minutes, or until juices run clear
   when tested with a knife.
5. Serve with barbecue sauce, honey
   mustard sauce, or ranch dressing
   for dipping.

Makes eight to ten servings.

When I was young I used to wait
On master and hand him his plate
Pass him the bottle when he got dry
And brush away the blue-tail fly

Chorus
Jimmy crack corn, and I don't care
Jimmy crack corn, and I don't care
Jimmy crack corn, and I don't care
My master's gone away

When he would ride in the afternoon
I'd follow him with my hickory broom
The pony being rather shy
When bitten by the blue-tail fly

Chorus

One day he rode around the farm
Flies so numerous that they did swarm

90

Blue-Tail Fly
(Jimmy Crack Corn)

One chanced to bite him on the thigh
The devil take the blue-tail fly

Chorus

Well the pony jumped, he start, he pitch
He threw my master in the ditch
He died and the jury wondered why
The verdict was the blue-tail fly

Chorus

Now he lies beneath the 'simmons tree
His epitaph is there to see
"Beneath this stone I'm forced to lie
The victim of the blue-tail fly"

Legendary Tall Tales: Sweet Betsy from Pike

during the Gold Rush of 1849, it seemed like the whole country had caught gold fever. Many pioneers loaded up their wagons, ready to brave terrible weather, sickness, and attacks by Native Americans and wild animals just for the chance to strike it rich in California.

The small community of Pike County, Missouri, was no different. Every day, more and more people were heading west. Betsy felt sad each time she saw more of her friends head off. Betsy was a spunky girl who desperately wanted to try her hand at gold panning and felt sure she'd be able to make a new life in California.

"Who knows what could be waiting for me in California?" she thought. "There's a whole world out there that's just begging to be explored."

Betsy tried to convince her parents to head west with the wagon trains, but they only laughed at her foolishness. Her father was a storekeeper and had a very successful business.

"Betsy, I *sell* my goods to those gold-hungry fools, I don't *join* them!" he told her.

But Betsy had her mind set for the golden land of California, and one day she got her chance to strike out.

Ike was a young man about Betsy's age who often helped Betsy's father in the store. One day, he didn't show up for work, and Betsy's father sent her to see what was keeping him. She found him loading up a small wagon with dry goods.

"And where are you off to? My father's pretty mad at you for not showing up this morning." Ike's yellow dog ran out and gave Betsy's hand a friendly lick.

Ike said, "I know that was wrong of me, but I'm setting off for California today. I can't let anything stop me."

"California, huh?" said Betsy. "And where'd you get these dry goods from?"

Ike turned bright red. "Well, your father was going to throw this stuff out anyway, so…"

Betsy saw her chance and jumped at it. "Listen, Ike, I don't want to tell my father about this, but the only way I'll keep quiet is if you take me to California with you."

Ike didn't want to take Betsy, but she fought so hard that he finally agreed to meet her that evening at midnight and set off.

Betsy was so excited to be heading to California that she barely felt sad at having to leave her home.

"It doesn't matter," she thought. "Soon I'll be so rich I'll be able to afford to send a message back home."

So Ike and Betsy set out, along with a pair of oxen, a spotted hog, a Shanghai rooster, and Ike's faithful yellow dog. For a while, things went very well for the two. Betsy had never had a chance to talk to Ike before, and she was amazed to hear his thoughts. He'd always been so quiet as he worked in her father's store.

Sleeping under the bright stars and breathing in the fresh prairie air of Nebraska, Betsy certainly thought this adventure was turning out very well.

She soon had cause to change her mind. The next day, a spoke on the wheel broke and they lost most of the day fixing it. A few days later, the rooster got sick, and they had to leave it behind.

"Not to worry," Betsy told Ike, "I'll make sure we wake up in the morning." She was trying to be optimistic, but things just seemed to get worse and worse. Next they tried to ford a river and most of their supplies were washed away. They were forced to eat the spotted hog. They trudged over the Sierra Mountains and both caught terrible colds. They couldn't take care of the cattle anymore, and were forced to leave them behind. They stumbled onward, only carrying the bare minimum of supplies on their backs.

"Betsy," Ike said as they made their way up another rocky slope, "I'm starting to think this might not have been such a good idea."

"Don't worry, Ike," Betsy answered. "It'll all be worth it when we reach California. I can almost see that gold now!"

But the worst was yet to come. Ike and Betsy reached the treacherous desert and almost gave up all hope. It stretched on for miles and miles and miles. It was so hot, images swam in front of Betsy. Her eyes burned with the glare and she was constantly rubbing sand out of them. They were running out of food and water, and even Ike's yellow dog ran away. "Can't say I blame him," Ike said sadly.

Just as they were about to give up entirely, the desert started to thin out. A few more miles, and they suddenly saw a small town on the horizon.

"Ike, we made it! We're in California!" Betsy cheered. They hugged and danced with joy. Then they started for the town. "Don't you see, Ike? Now I can finally begin my adventures!"

Ike looked so sad that Betsy stopped short. "You look like a fella that just lost his best horse. What's the matter?"

"Now that we're in California and you're ready to begin your adventures, I guess you won't have any need for a boy from back home like me," he said in a small voice.

Betsy was shocked. She'd been around Ike for so long, they'd shared so many experiences, she couldn't imagine her life without him. Suddenly, she realized how much Ike meant to her.

"Ike, the only adventures I want to have are with you by my side," she declared, and Ike thought his heart would burst in two.

Ike and Betsy got married that very week. Some said they found gold in the California hills, and some said that they ended up fighting when Ike got jealous of all the attention the miners gave Betsy. But one thing was clear: sweet Betsy from Pike was never at a loss for adventures ever again! 🏃

Did you ever hear tell of
Sweet Betsy from Pike,
Who crossed the wide prairies
With her husband, Ike,
With two yoke of cattle
And one spotted hog,
A tall shanghai rooster,
And an old yeller dog?

Sing toorali—oorali—oorali ay!
Sing toorali—oorali—oorali ay!

The alkali desert
Was burning and bare
And Ike cried in fear,
"We are lost, I declare!
My dear old Pike County,
I'll go back to you."
Said Betsy, "You'll go by yourself,
If you do."

Sweet Betsy from Pike

Sing toorali—oorali—oorali ay!
Sing toorali—oorali—oorali ay!

They swam the wide rivers
And crossed the tall peaks
They camped on the prairie
For weeks upon weeks.
They fought off the Indians
With musket and ball
And reached California
In spite of it all.

Sing toorali—oorali—oorali ay!
Sing toorali—oorali—oorali ay!

Things to Think

BY ROBERT BLY

Think in ways you've never thought before
If the phone rings, think of it as carrying a message
Larger than anything you've ever heard,
Vaster than a hundred lines of Yeats.

Think that someone may bring a bear to your door,
Maybe wounded and deranged; or think that a moose
Has risen out of the lake, and he's carrying on his antlers
A child of your own whom you've never seen.

When someone knocks on the door, think that he's about
To give you something large: tell you you're forgiven,
Or that it's not necessary to work all the time, or that it's
Been decided that if you lie down no one will die.

The Two Goats on The Bridge

Two goats that were each trying to cross a stream met in the middle of the bridge. The bridge wasn't wide enough for either goat to pass the other, so one said, "This plank won't hold us both. Let me by and then you can go on your way." But the other replied, "Why should I move? Why don't you step off the bridge and let me pass?" They argued like this for an hour, each one not letting the other pass, until finally they began pushing and fighting. Suddenly, the plank broke and both of the goats fell into the freezing water.

Moral: Don't be as stubborn as goats!

The Camptown ladies sing their song,
Doodah, doodah!
The Camptown racetrack's five miles long,
Oh, doodah day!

I come down here with my hat caved in,
Doodah, doodah!
I go back home with a pocket full of tin.
Oh, doodah day!

Chorus
Goin' to run all night, Goin' to run all day.
I'll bet my money on a bobtail nag;
Somebody bet on the bay.

Camptown Races

The longtail filly and the big black horse,
Doodah, doodah!
They fly the track and they both cut across,
Oh, dooday day!

The blind horse stickin' in a big mud hole,
Doodah, doodah!
Can't touch bottom with a ten foot pole
Oh, doodah day!

Chorus

Papa's Pasta Secrets

When cooking pasta, it's easy to plan ahead for fast-food dining. Just toss an extra serving or two of noodles into the pot. Once the pasta is cooked and drained, store the extra noodles in an airtight container. Stir the pasta with a bit of oil to prevent the noodles from sticking, then refrigerate. No cooking necessary for tomorrow's lunch or dinner: Just heat up the left-over pasta and sauce, and call it a meal.

String Pie

1 pound ground beef,
1/2 cup finely chopped onion
1/4 cup green pepper, diced
16 ounces favorite pasta sauce
8 ounces spaghetti, cooked
and drained
1/3 cup grated Parmesan cheese
2 eggs, beaten
1 tablespoon softened butter
1 cup cottage cheese
1/2 cup shredded mozzarella cheese

1. Preheat oven to 350°F.
2. In large skillet, cook beef, onion, and green pepper until meat is completely browned. Drain excess fat. Stir in pasta sauce.
3. In large bowl, combine pasta, Parmesan cheese, eggs, and butter until thoroughly mixed.
4. Transfer noodle mixture to 9- by 13-inch baking dish. Spread cottage cheese evenly over the top. Cover with sauce. Sprinkle top with mozzarella cheese.
5. Bake for 20 minutes, or until pie is heated through and cheese is melted.

Makes six servings.

Fettuccine Alfredo

3/4 pound fettuccine
5 tablespoons butter
2/3 cup whipping cream
1/4 teaspoon salt,
Dash white pepper
Dash nutmeg
1 cup grated Parmesan cheese
2 tablespoons chopped fresh parsley

1. Cook pasta and set aside in large saucepan.
2. In a heavy skillet over medium heat, warm up butter and cream until bubbling. Stir for 2 minutes, then stir in salt, pepper, and nutmeg. Remove from heat.
3. Stir cheese into mixture until sauce is smooth.
4. Pour sauce over noodles. Toss over low heat for 2 to 3 minutes until fettuccine is thoroughly coated and sauce is thickened.
5. Serve with fresh parsley on top.

Makes four servings.

No-Fuss Ravioli-Spinach Lasagna

Nonstick vegetable spray
1 (26-ounce) jar pasta sauce
1 (30-ounce) package of frozen cheese ravioli
1 (10-ounce) package of frozen spinach, thawed and squeezed dry
8 ounces shredded mozzarella cheese
1/2 cup grated Parmesan cheese

1. Preheat oven to 350°F.
2. Coat a 9- by 13-inch baking pan with cooking spray.
3. Spoon a third of the sauce into pan, then layer half the ravioli and all the spinach on top. Add half the mozzarella and half the Parmesan cheese. Top with the remaining ravioli, sauce, and cheese.
4. Cover pan with aluminum foil and bake for 25 minutes.
5. Remove foil and bake for an additional 5 to 10 minutes, or until cheese is bubbly.

Makes six servings.

Legendary Tall Tales: The Mighty Big Story of Paul Bunyan

Once upon a time, there lived a very famous lumberjack named Paul Bunyan. Now, when Paul was born, he looked like any other baby. But he started growing at an amazing pace, and within a week, he had to wear his father's clothes. By the time he was a child, he had to use wagon wheels for buttons!

Paul Bunyan grew bigger and bigger, until finally his family began to worry that they wouldn't be able to afford to feed and clothe him anymore.

"Now son," his father said, "you know we love you, but, well, it looks like you're getting a little too large for this family." He had to use a megaphone so Paul could hear his words that high up in the air. "Maybe it's time you stepped out and had a look at this great big country."

"Oh Paul." His mother wept and stepped into his hand so he could bring her up to his face for a kiss. Paul hated leaving his little family, but he knew they were right. Ever since he was little, something in his heart wouldn't let him feel satisfied. Maybe if he went out into the wide world, he might find out what it was he wanted someday.

Saying goodbye was hard, but he was careful not to cry—otherwise he would have flooded the entire area! Paul promised to keep in touch, and then he packed up his few belongings and strode off into the wilderness. The ground shook with each giant step he took.

After walking for a while, Paul started to feel very sad and lonely. He lay down on the ground and looked up into the deep blue sky. "This wouldn't be so bad," he thought, "if I only had a friend to travel with me." He drifted off to sleep, but suddenly woke up when he felt something rough and wet on his face. He opened his eyes and was amazed to find a giant ox licking him. Not only was the ox as big as Paul, but he was bright blue as well, as if he had just stepped down from out of the sky! Paul had no idea how he had come there, but he was grateful for a friend. He named the ox Babe, and from that day forth, the two were inseparable.

The pair traveled all over the country, shaping it wherever they went. Their giant footprints became the 10,000 lakes of Minnesota when they filled with rainwater. And he dug out the Grand Canyon just so he and Babe could take a bath!

Weather was odd back then, and one

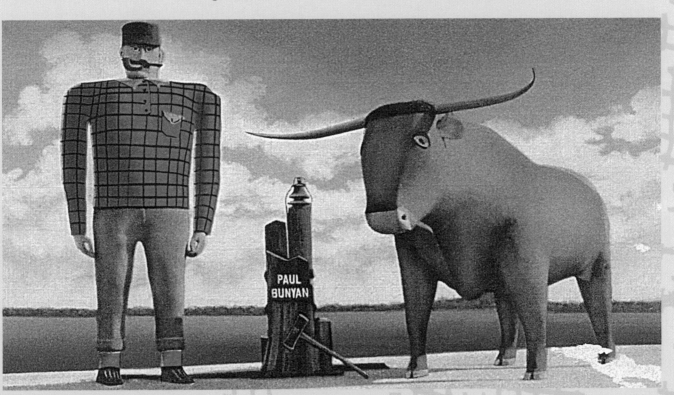

year the country had two winters. Because his head was as high as a mountaintop, Paul found he couldn't make a sound since his words froze stiff as soon as they came out of his mouth. It wasn't until the spring that his words thawed, and then the air rang with his chatter for a whole week! Paul and Babe thought this was so funny that they fell on the ground and rolled from side to side, and that's how the Black Hills of South Dakota were formed.

Yes, Paul was certainly having a grand time with Babe, but he still was not content and he couldn't exactly say why.

One day, as he was strolling through Oregon picking up huge boulders as if they were pebbles and skipping them across lakes, he walked right into the middle of a loggers' camp. All of the men were startled to see giant Paul, but they were so busy worrying that they barely shouted out a greeting.

"Hey, you," Paul called to a man by his feet. "Why's everyone so glum?"

The man said, "We're all worried about our jobs. We're supposed to cut down two hundred trees by tomorrow, but everyone's sick with the whooping cough and can't work." He wrung his hands. "We're all going to get fired, and then what will we tell our families?'

"Two hundred trees, huh?" Paul said, half to himself. "Why, I bet I could cut down those trees for you in about two hours."

Then, taking two of the giant blades from a woodcutting machine, he fashioned two axes and set off for the forest. "Come on, Babe!" he called, "we've got work to do!"

And work they did. All you could hear for miles around was the *Woosh!* of Paul's axes whistling through the air and the *Crash!* as trees fell. Although he cut down an incredible amount, he was careful to leave the young trees to grow, and he didn't harm any of the other parts of the forest. Babe caught all of the logs Paul tossed to him on his broad back and tugged them into a pile.

Before Paul had even broken a sweat, there were the two hundred logs, neatly stacked and ready to go. All of the men from the logging camp cheered!

"Thanks Paul!" they all called up.

Paul smiled to himself at the work he had done. "You know, Babe, I think this might just be the job for me." And so he stayed on at the logging camp, helping to clear the forest and produce wood for the growing country. No one could beat Paul Bunyan in any contest of strength, and he and Babe always had the most logs cut by the end of the day.

Paul made a lot of friends at the logging camp and had a good time traveling with them. In fact, the only one who sometimes grumbled was the cook. In order to make Paul's flapjacks, he had to heat up a skillet a mile long, and then have ten men strap pats of butter to their feet to grease it! Twenty men had to work together to flip each flapjack, and then Paul would come along and eat them all up in about a minute! The cook would fling up his hands and take to his bed for the rest of the day, but everyone else in the camp thought this was hilarious.

And so, Paul Bunyan finally felt satisfied as he worked hard with his blue ox and his friends from the camps. The stories about him grew and grew, much like Paul did when he was a little boy, until finally his were the tallest tales of all! 🏃

A Fairy Tale Verse

Everyone was fast asleep,
Princess, courtiers, cats and sheep,
And there grew a thorny wall
Through which none could come at all.
Thus a hundred years rolled past
Till a royal prince at last
Cut his way through thorns, and they
Turned to roses right away.

Sleeping Beauty

Then he kissed the princess's eyes
And she woke in sweet surprise.
Soon the palace was astir,
Ready to rejoice with her.

ACTIVITIES

Capture a Spider Web

Spider webs are fragile wonders of nature, as you and your grandchildren know if you've ever tried to touch one only to find the silk strands whisked away into the wind or nearby branches. If you happen upon an abandoned orb web or sheet web, here's a way to capture its beauty and intricate details without getting sticky fingers.

Black cardboard, spray glue or hair spray, small manicure scissors

The secret to success with this project is patience and gentleness. Some webs may be trickier than others to capture, so try to locate several spider webs in advance. That way, if one comes apart, your grandchild can try again. Start by cutting a black piece of cardboard a few inches larger in diameter than the spider web you want to collect. Spray one side of the cardboard lightly with glue or hair spray. Hold the sticky side up to the web, then slowly and gently press the cardboard against the web until all strands are touching it. Use the small manicure scissors to carefully detach the spider web from its support branches. Now you can carry the web away.

SPIDER HOMES

■ Not all spiders live in webs. Primitive ones, such as trapdoor spiders, baboon spiders, and tarantulas live in **SILK-LINED BURROWS** in the ground. Each year, as trapdoor spiders grow, they add another silk rim to their door. You can tell the age of the spider based on the number of rims.

- Garden spiders, such as the golden silk spider, the black-and-yellow garden spider, and the marbled spider, build spiral-shaped orb webs. You can find circular **ORB WEBS**, spun in rays and spirals of silk, in sunny places outdoors around buildings, gardens, and tall grasses.

- Grass spiders build **FUNNEL WEBS**. These weavers build horizontal sheet-like webs with a tornado-shaped funnel in the grass. These webs are most obvious in the morning when glistening with dew. The funnel serves as a hiding place for the spider as she awaits her prey.

- Small, dark, and shiny **SHEET WEB** spiders are nocturnal hunters that weave small, horizontal sheets of webbing that can be flat or dome-shaped. They're among the biggest spider families in the world and are found in all kinds of habitats.

- **COBWEB** spiders, such as the red-bellied black widow or the long-legged cellar spider, build irregular webs out of soft and fluffy silk both outdoors and indoors in protected places. These spiders tend to hang upside down in their webs.

- **TRIANGLE WEB** spiders spin three-sided, triangular webs. The spider waits for prey on one corner. When an insect lands on the web, the spider shakes it until the insect gets caught in the sticky silk.

Food Jokes

Why did the mother tell the baby ghost when he ate too fast?

Stop goblin your food.

How many sandwiches can you eat on an empty stomach?

One. After the first, your stomach is no longer empty

What two things are never eaten for breakfast?

Lunch and dinner.

Why did the orange stop?

Because it ran out of juice.

Why did the student eat his homework?

The teacher told him it was a piece of cake.

What's the worst thing about being an octopus?

Washing your hands before dinner.

What starts with a "t," ends with a "t," and is full of "t"?

A teapot.

When do you stop at green, and go at red?

When you're eating a watermelon.

How do you make an egg laugh?

Tell it a yolk.

HERE IN BRAND~NEW HAT AND TIE-
IS MISTER JAKE McPHLISTER.

TURN THE PICTURE ROUND ABOUT
AND SEE HIS CHARMING SISTER!

From the great Atlantic Ocean
To the wide Pacific shore,
From sunny California
To ice-bound Labrador,
She's mighty tall and handsome,
She's known quite well by all,
She's the 'boes' accommodation
On the Wabash Cannonball!

Chorus
Listen to the jingle,
The rumble and the roar,
As she glides along the woodlands,
Through hills and by the shore
Hear the mighty rush of the engine,
Hear those lonesome hoboes squawl,
While traveling through the jungle
On the Wabash Cannonball

She came down from Birmingham
One cold December day,
As she rolled into the station,
You could hear the people say,
There's a girl from Birmingham,
She's long and she is tall,
She come down from Birmingham on
The Wabash Cannonball

Chorus

This train, she runs to Memphis,
Mattoon, and Mexico.
She rolls through East St. Louis
And she never does it slow,
As she flies through Colorado,
She gives an awful squawl,
They tell her by her whistle
The Wabash Cannonball

Chorus

Our eastern states are dandy,
So the people always say,
From New York to St. Louis
And Chicago by the way,
From the hills of Minnesota
Where the rippling waters fall,
No changes can be taken
On the Wabash Cannonball

Chorus

Now here's to Boston Blackey,
May his name forever stand,
And always be remembered
By the 'boes throughout the land,
His earthly days are over
And the curtains 'round him fall,
We'll carry him home to victory
On the Wabash Cannonball

The Wabash Cannonball

Grandfather Wisdoms

The time is always ripe for doing right.
—MARTIN LUTHER KING, JR.

■

A clean conscience makes a soft pillow.

■

No act of kindness, no
matter how small,
is ever wasted.
—AESOP

■

No one is useless in this world who
lightens the burden of others.
—CHARLES DICKENS

■

Always do right. This will gratify
some people and astonish the rest.
—MARK TWAIN

Three things in human life are important: the first is to be kind. The second is to be kind. The third is to be kind.

—HENRY JAMES

■

Deal with yourself as an individual worthy of respect, and make everyone else deal with you the same way.

—NIKKI GIOVANNI

■

Let every man be respected as an individual and no man idolized.

—ALBERT EINSTEIN

■

Never bend your head. Always hold it high. Look the world straight in the eye.

—HELEN KELLER

LEGENDARY TALL TALES: SALLY ANN THUNDER ANN WHIRLWIND MEETS HER MATCH

1iving on the frontier was a very difficult life. People were always so busy hunting or farming or protecting themselves that there wasn't much time for fun. But every once in awhile, pioneers would polish themselves up and have a rip-roarin' barn dance. Boys and girls would often meet at these dances and fall in love— wedding bells wouldn't be too far behind.

Sally Ann Thunder Ann Whirlwind didn't give a hoot about wedding bells, however. As her name suggested, pretty Sally Ann was full of energy and spirit. She boasted she could outrun a jackrabbit, outwit a fox, and outwrestle any man in town. Supposedly, Sally Ann's voice was so powerful that she once screamed the feathers off an eagle's head, and that's how the bald eagle came to be. But she could also be enchanting. Once she charmed the skin right off a bear one cold winter. She wore a bee's nest as a Sunday bonnet and could often be seen running with wolves through the woods.

It was during one such excursion in the woods that she came across a hilarious sight. A man had somehow gotten his head stuck between two closely growing tree trunks and could not free himself!

"What do you think you're doing?" she asked between giggles.

The man was in no mood for jokes and answered angrily, "What does it look like? I fell asleep beneath these trees and somehow got my head stuck. I think the raccoons are playing a trick on me." He tugged again at his head, but it was stuck fast. "Well, are you going to help me or just stand there like a silly fool?"

Sally Ann didn't like his tone, but agreed to help. Quickly she found two long snakes and tied them together. Then, looping one over a trunk, she pulled back with all her might until the tree bent enough for the man to remove his head.

The man dusted off his raccoon-skin hat and started to walk away.

"Didn't anyone teach you any manners?" Sally Ann called after him, but he had already disappeared.

When she got back to the village, everyone was very excited about the barn dance that night. Sally Ann loved dancing, but she despised the fact that every single boy in the village had requested her as a date. Couldn't she just go by herself and have a good time? Finally she declared to her mother, "The only man who will be my partner is the man who can outdance me at the party!" And she meant it. So Sally Ann showed up by herself, looking as beautiful and fresh as a wild rose.

The first boy to ask her to dance was confident Tim Palmer. He thought he'd have no trouble keeping up with Sally Ann, but two fast jigs tuckered him out, and as soon as he stopped for a moment, another boy, John Walker, took his place. John only lasted two dances. After that, a string of boys danced with Sally Ann, but each gave up, until only Sally Ann was left, still looking fresh and not even out of breath. She was just about to request a drink, when a voice piped up next to her.

"Might I try my hand at a dance with you?" She looked over to see the man with the raccoon-skin hat that she had rescued that morning.

"Oh, I see you suddenly learned some manners." She sniffed.

The man gave a sheepish grin. "Pardon me for this morning, miss. I was so embarrassed by my predicament that I just couldn't bear facing such a lovely creature as yourself." He stuck out his hand, "Allow me to introduce myself. My name's Davy Crockett. And you must be the famous Sally Ann Thunder Ann Whirlwind."

Sally Ann was amazed. Davy Crockett was a famous frontiersman, and here he was, asking her for a dance! But she

124

remembered how rude he'd been that morning, and decided not to go easy on him during the next jig.

"I accept, Mr. Crockett," she said, ignoring his hand. "Let's hope your dancing is better then your manners." *After all,* she thought, *what would a frontiersman know about dancing?*

But Sally Ann was in for the surprise of her life. Davy Crockett's feet moved so fast that they were practically a blur. She tried all of her most complicated steps, but Davy Crockett kept up with each one. One, two, three dances went by. She could see the sweat standing on his forehead, but Davy Crocket never stopped smiling and never stopped dancing.

"Had enough?" she managed to gasp.

"Why, I'm just getting started," he said.

They danced like dervishes through the entire night and even into the next day! People were so amazed by the spectacle that they forgot to go to sleep. Sally Ann knew she couldn't keep it up forever. Suddenly, her ankle twisted and she fell forward. Quick as a wink, Davy Crockett shot out an arm and caught her.

"You win!" she cried, knowing that she had finally met her match.

Davy smiled at her. "Good. One more jig, and I would've been a goner."

Sally Ann and Davy Crockett soon married. Sally Ann never quit being feisty, but whenever she acted a little too stubborn, Davy would take out a fiddle and play a little dance tune, to remind her how he bested her fair and square. And whenever Davy forgot his manners, Sally Ann would look for a pair of good strong trees to stick his head between.

"And maybe this time," she'd laughingly tell him, "There won't be any snakes around to save you!"

Dreams

BY ELLA YOUNG

I went sailing
Over the sea,
White gulls and grey gulls
Following me.

Pale sea-palaces
Under my prow,
Trees with gold apples
On every bough!

Golden fishes,
Silver and blue,
Swam before me
Two and two,

Till a wave of Faery,
Curling white,
Whelmed my boat
In rainbow light.

The Oak & The Weeds

A mighty, proud oak tree was uprooted during a storm and fell into a brook. It floated downstream until it came to rest beside a patch of weeds. "Isn't that strange?" thought the oak. "These weeds are weak and small and yet they have survived the storm. I am a strong oak, and yet the storm has torn me up by the roots!" A weed that had heard the oak replied, "It is because you are so proud and stiff that you were blown down. We weeds bow and yield to the wind, and so we remain standing even after you have fallen."

Moral: Sometimes it is better to bend and be flexible than to remain stiff and stubborn.

The Boy & The Cookie Jar

A little boy reached into a cookie jar to grab some chocolate-chip cookies, which were his favorite. They looked so delicious that instead of just taking one, he grabbed a handful. But when he tried to pull his hand out, he realized that the opening was too small and his hand was stuck. Again and again he tried to pull the cookies up, but it was no use. He was about to start crying when his mother came in and saw his situation. "If you had only taken one, you could have pulled your hand out easily and would be munching on that cookie right now! Instead, you don't have any by trying to take too many at once," she told him.

Moral: It is better to have a little than none at all.

129

One-Dish Wonders

The next time your grandchildren are over for dinner, surprise them with your quick kitchen finesse. Instead of ordering takeout chicken, Thai, or stir-fried rice, try these recipes for homemade substitutes that can be made faster than the time it takes for delivery. You can probably find most of the ingredients in your pantry already. In a half hour or less, you can have a hot meal on the table, with minimal cleanup. Now that's cooking, Grandpa-style!

Hoppin' John Supper

1 cup uncooked white rice
1 (15-ounce) can chicken broth
$1/4$ cup water
1 (16-ounce) package frozen black-eyed peas, thawed
1 tablespoon vegetable oil
1 cup chopped onion
1 cup diced carrot
$3/4$ cup celery, thinly sliced, with tops
3 cloves garlic, minced)
12 ounces fully-cooked lean ham, cut into $3/4$-inch cubes
1 teaspoon hot pepper sauce
$1/2$ teaspoon salt
2 tablespoons fresh chopped parsley

1. In large saucepan, combine rice, chicken broth, and water. Bring to a boil over high heat. Reduce heat and simmer, covered, for 10 minutes.
2. Stir in peas, then cover and simmer for 10 minutes more, or until peas are tender and liquid is absorbed.
3. In the meantime, heat oil in a large skillet over medium heat. Sauté onions, carrots, celery, and garlic for about 10 minutes, until vegetables are tender.
4. Add ham to veggies and heat through.
5. Stir in rice-and-bean mixture, pepper sauce, and salt.

6. Cover and cook over low heat for 10 minutes.
7. Sprinkle top with parsley and serve hot.

Makes six servings.

Easy Thai Satay

1/2 cup creamy peanut butter
2 teaspoons lite soy sauce
2 teaspoons balsamic vinegar
1 tablespoon fresh lemon juice
1-ounce package of roasted-garlic salad dressing mix
3/4 cup water
1 pound sirloin, sliced and pounded thin
1 tablespoon sesame oil
Wooden skewers (presoaked in water to prevent them from scorching)

1. Preheat broiler.
2. In a small bowl, whisk together dipping sauce of peanut butter, soy sauce, vinegar, lemon juice, 1 tablespoon salad dressing mix, and water. Set aside.
3. In a large bowl, mix remaining salad dressing mix and sesame oil. Stir in sirloin strips until they are thoroughly coated.
4. Skewer each strip of beef and broil for 2 to 3 minutes per side.
5. Serve hot with the dipping sauce and enjoy!

Quick "Fried" Chicken

Nonstick vegetable spray
2 cups instant potato flakes
1 whole chicken, cut up, with skin removed, or 3 to 4 pounds chicken parts
1 cup ranch salad dressing

1. Preheat oven to 450°F.
2. Coat a baking sheet with non-stick vegetable spray.

3. Pour potato flakes onto a large plate or into a large bowl. Brush each piece of chicken with ranch dressing, then roll in potato flakes until completely coated.

4. Arrange chicken pieces on baking sheet and place in oven.

5. Turn oven down to 350° F and bake for 25 minutes, or until juices run clear when poked with a fork.

Makes four servings.

I Shall Not Pass This Way Again

ANONYMOUS

Through this toilsome world, alas!

Once and only once I pass;

If a kindness I may show,

If a good deed I may do

To a suffering fellow man,

Let me do it while I can.

No delay, for it is plain

I shall not pass this way again.

Tiny Boats

Amaze your grandkids with these funny little boats that can be made from almost anything! An empty walnut shell or a broken eggshell can easily become a seafaring vessel. Even the smallest children can make an aluminum-foil boat, and a peanut canoe looks so realistic you won't believe how quick it is to make. Complete your fleet of homemade boats with some matchstick people, and send them sailing the next time there's a rainy day.

WALNUT OR EGGSHELL BOAT

Make a sail by drawing a design or picture on a small piece of paper using crayons or markers. Make two small slits at the top and bottom, and then weave a toothpick through the slits to create a mast. Use craft glue or a small piece of craft gum to attach the toothpick mast to the inside at one end of half a walnut shell for a tiny one-man sea cruiser. You could also use one half of a clean eggshell.

ALUMINUM-FOIL BOAT

Start with a piece of foil approximately 6 inches square. Fold the square in half and slightly scrunch and pinch the two ends closed. Reopen the boat gently. Stand the boat on a flat surface and use your fingers to flatten the bottom down a little so it will float.

PEANUT CANOE

Cut the top off of a large peanut shell lengthwise, making sure to leave the ends on. Remove the peanut to hollow out the inside. Add a brave little matchstick sailor, and your peanut canoe is ready for action!

MATCHSTICK PEOPLE

Remove a match from a matchbook. Using a pair of scissors, cut a slit in the bottom to about halfway up and slightly separate the two pieces. Be careful not to break them. These will be the legs. Carefully make two slits on either side of the matchstick from the middle up to a little bit before the matchstick head. These will be the arms. Gently fold the legs to make your matchstick

A Fairy Tale Verse

Cinderella sits in tears
Till the fairy dame appears;
Then in satin, after all,
Off she flutters to the ball.
There she has a lovely time
Till the bells at midnight chime;
Hastily she runs to find

Cinderella

For her coach a pumpkin rind;
But her shoe, left on the stair,
No one in the world can wear
Save the kitchen maiden, who
Makes the prince's dream come true.

There's a dark and a troubled side of life,
There's a bright and a sunny side, too;
Though you meet with the
  darkness and strife,
The sunny side may also find you.

Chorus
Keep on the sunny side, always on the sunny side,
Keep on the sunny side of life;
It will help us ev'ry day, it will brighten all the way,
If we keep on the sunny side of life

Oh, the storm and its fury broke today,
Crushing hopes that we cherish so dear;
Clouds and storms will in time pass away,
The sun again will shine bright and clear.

140

Chorus

Let us greet with a song of hope each day,
Though the moment be cloudy or fair;
Let us trust in our Saviour away,
Who keepeth ev'ry one in His care.

Chorus

Keep On the Sunny Side

141

TEN LITTLE PUPPY DOGS

TEN little puppy dogs painting on a sign,
One got painted out---then there were NINE.

NINE little puppy dogs writing on a slate,
One was subtracted--- then there were EIGHT.

EIGHT little puppy dogs playing "odd and even",
One got counted out---then there were SEVEN.

SEVEN little puppy dogs playing circus tricks,
One barked himself away-- then there were SIX.

SIX little puppy dogs playing with a hive,
Busy bees drove one off---then there were FIVE.

FIVE little puppy dogs going to the store,
One lost his little self---then there were FOUR.

FOUR little puppy dogs sailing o'er the sea,
One swam away to shore---then there were THREE.

THREE little puppy dogs bought a pot of glue,
One got stuck to a pig---then there were TWO.

TWO little puppy dogs snoozing in the sun,
One dreamed he was a bone---then there was ONE.

ONE little puppy dog hunting for a penny,
He got lost himself --- then there wasn't ANY!

Taco Temptations

Taco dinners make festive meals—and stuffing their own tortilla shells is ideal for picky eaters who like to play with their food! Traditional tacos often feature shredded or ground beef spiced up with taco seasoning, topped with shredded cheese, tomatoes, lettuce, olives, guacamole, and sour cream. Some of the following regional variations may be off the beaten path for many taco lovers, but once you try them, they might become the new standard at your dinner table.

SoCal Fish Tacos

$1/2$ cup sour cream
$1/2$ cup mayonnaise
$1/4$ cup cilantro, finely chopped
1 (1.25-ounce) package taco
seasoning mix
$1/8$ cup fresh-squeezed lime juice
1 pound cod fillets, cut into
1-inch pieces
2 tablespoons vegetable oil
2 tablespoons lemon juice
12 taco shells
$1^{1}/2$ cups shredded cabbage
2 tomatoes, chopped

1. In small bowl, whisk together sour cream, mayonnaise, cilantro, 2 tablespoons taco seasoning, and lime juice.
2. In medium bowl, stir cod pieces, oil, lemon juice, and remaining taco seasoning together. Pour contents into large skillet and cook over medium-high heat. Stir frequently for about 5 minutes, until fish flakes easily when tested with fork.
3. Fill taco shells with fish mixture and add cabbage and tomatoes Top with sour-cream blend. Serve immediately.

Makes twelve servings.

Southwestern Chicken Tacos

Nonstick cooking spray
12 ounces chicken breast,
cut into small pieces
1 cup salsa
1 (7-ounce) can Mexican-style
corn, drained
$1/2$ cup canned black beans, drained
8 taco shells
$1^1/2$ cups shredded lettuce
$1/2$ cup shredded cheddar cheese or
Mexican white cheese
1 tomato, chopped
Sour cream

1. Coat large skillet with cooking spray and heat over medium flame. Add chicken and $1/2$ cup salsa, and cook for about 5 minutes, stirring frequently, until chicken is cooked through.
2. Stir in corn and beans, and simmer for about 3 minutes, until mixture is slightly reduced.
3. Spoon chicken mixture into taco shells. Top with lettuce, cheese, tomato, and remaining salsa. Add a dollop of sour cream, if desired.

Makes eight servings.

Picadillo Salsa

3 large ripe tomatoes, cored
and chopped
1 medium red onion, chopped
$1/2$ bunch cilantro, finely chopped
3 jalapeño peppers, cored and finely
chopped (you might want to wear
gloves for this to avoid getting
pepper juice on skin)
$1/4$ cup fresh-squeezed lime juice
Sea salt to taste

1. In medium-size bowl, stir all ingredients together until blended.
2. Adjust ingredients to personal taste and serve with tacos or as dip for tortilla chips.

Makes about two cups.

Very Veggie Tacos

1 tablespoon vegetable oil
1 medium onion, thinly sliced
1 green pepper, thinly sliced
1 hot serrano pepper, thinly sliced (you might want to wear gloves for this to avoid getting pepper juice on skin)
1 medium zucchini, thinly sliced
1/2 cup water
1 clove garlic, minced
2 1/2 cups beans (black, refried, or pinto)
1 large tomato, chopped
Sea salt to taste
8 taco shells
Sour cream
Taco sauce

1. In large skillet, sauté onion and peppers in hot oil over medium heat until tender.
2. Add zucchini and cook for about 5 minutes more.
3. Add 1/4 cup water and garlic. Bring mixture to a simmer.
4. Add beans and remaining water and bring mixture to a boil.
5. When mixture is heated through and has reached desired consistency, remove from heat. Stir in tomatoes. Add salt to taste.
6. Spoon veggie mixture into taco shells. Garnish each with dollop of sour cream and dash of taco sauce, if desired.

Makes eight servings.

Who Has Seen the Wind?

BY CHRISTINA ROSSETTI

Who has seen the wind?
  Neither I nor you:
But when the leaves hand trembling,
  The wind is passing through.

Who has seen the wind?
  Neither you nor I:
But when the trees bow down their heads,
  The wind is passing by.

The Blue Jay
& The Owl

One day, an old barn owl had a visit from his good friend, the blue jay. The owl sat quietly in a little corner while the blue jay talked about all the things he was doing and all of the other birds he had visited. In fact, the blue jay talked so much that the owl did not say a single word the entire time! After an hour of talking nonstop, the blue jay fluffed up his feathers and said goodbye. "Dear owl, I can't remember the last time I had such a wonderful conversation with someone! You've cheered me up so much!" he called as he flew away.

Moral: Sometimes all you need to do is sit still and listen.

The Cat, The Mouse & The Rooster

One day a very young mouse came home and said, "I saw the most terrible thing in the garden! It strutted about on two legs and was as black as coal. It wore a red flag on its head, and a red scarf tied around its throat, and it flapped its arms up and down in a very alarming way. It stretched its neck out and roared at me until I thought it would eat me up! It made me shake from head to foot and I ran home as fast as I could!" The little mouse sighed. "And what's even worse was that I was just about to make friends with a very pretty creature! She had soft, dark fur like ours, and a long tail, and appeared so friendly that I'm positive we would have been good friends. She looked at me with her bright eyes and opened her mouth, and I'm sure she was about to speak to me when that horrible creature started raising a racket and I ran away!"

An old mouse shook his head. "My dear child, the noisy creature you saw was only a rooster, and roosters have always gotten along with mice. But the pretty thing you were so fond of was a cat, and cats eat mice !"

Moral: Don't judge others by their appearance.

A Fairy Tale Verse

Two little children, dear and good,
Were sent to wander in the wood,
Because their uncle, bad and bold,
Desired to seize their goods and gold;
For since they seemed so sweet and pretty
He spared their young lives out of pity.
Afraid, for days they trudged about
Till hungry, cold, and quite tired out,

Babes in the Wood

Within the lonesome forest deep
The babes lay down and fell asleep,
And then the kindly robins spread
A quilt of leaves upon their bed.

155

HERE'S A GENTLE MOOLY COW
BY AN UPRIGHT LOG

UPSIDE DOWN

DOWNSIDE UP

TURN THE PICTURE ROUND LIKE THIS
AND FIND A FUNNY FROG

Jokes Animal

What time is it when an elephant sits on a fence?

Time to fix the fence.

How do you keep an elephant from charging?

Take away his credit card.

How do porcupines play leap-frog?

Very carefully!

Who says "quick, quick"?

A duck with the hiccups.

What did the pony say when he coughed?

"Pardon me, I'm a little horse."

What's the difference between a flea and a coyote?

One prowls on the hairy, the other howls on the prairie.

Why do they put bells on cows?

Because their horns don't blow.

Why was the baby ant so confused?

Because all of his uncles were ants.

What's the best way to catch a squirrel?

Climb a tree and act like a nut.

Oh, give me a home, where the buffalo roam,
Where the deer and the antelope play;
Where seldom is heard a discouraging word,
And the skies are not cloudy all day.

Chorus
Home, home on the range,
Where the deer and the antelope play;
Where seldom is heard a discouraging word,
And the skies are not cloudy all day.

How often at night when the heavens are bright
With the lights from the glittering stars;
Have I stood there amazed and asked as I gazed
If their glory exceeds that of ours.

Chorus

Oh, give me a land where the bright diamond sand
Flows leisurely down the stream;
Where the graceful, white swan goes gliding along,
Like a maid in a heavenly dream.

Chorus

Where the air is so pure, the zephyrs so free,
The breezes so balmy and light,

Home On the Range

That I would not exchange my home on
 the range
For all of the cities so bright.

Chorus

Oh, I love those wild flowers in this dear land of ours,
The curlew I love to hear scream,
And I love the white rocks and the antelope flocks
That graze on the mountain tops green.

Chorus

A Fairy Tale Verse

You know the puss of clever pate
Who made his master rich and great:
First to the king he sent some game
And tagged it with his master's name;
Then when the king was passing by,
"These are my *master's* fields!" he'd cry;
A giant (in disguise a mouse)
He ate, and seized the giant's house,

Puss in Boots

Where, boasting it his lord's domain
The king he begged to entertain.
All this, of course, was sure to please,
And Puss, henceforward, lived in ease.

Simple Camp Cooking

One of the best things about making the perfect campfire is the mouthwatering smell of campfire cooking. Whether heading out for an early fishing expedition or hike through the woods, sunrise hearty hash is sure to please the taste buds and give you a good head start on the day. Chuckwagon burgers cook in minutes, and with the added corn chips in the mix, buns are optional. Sweet, fresh summer corn is cooked to perfection over hot coals, and the best part is that it comes in its own cooking wrapper. And as the campfire dies down to a golden glow, it becomes just the right temperature for making yummy roasted-apple pockets.

Sunrise Hearty Hash

2 large potatoes
1 onion
Water
1 tablespoon mustard
Salt, to taste
Pepper, to taste
A few dashes Tabasco sauce
1 12-ounce can corned beef
4 eggs, cooked sunny side up

1. Dice the potatoes and onions and combine in a large skillet. Add enough water to cover the potatoes and onions, and stir in mustard, salt, pepper, Tabasco sauce.
2. Allow the mixture to simmer over medium coals until almost tender.
3. Stir in the corned beef and adjust the seasonings if necessary. Continue to simmer uncovered until the mixture is tender and of the desired consistency.
4. Serve on a platter and top with a sunny-side-up egg.

Makes four servings.

Chuckwagon Burgers

*1¹/₂ pounds ground beef, ground
turkey, or veggie burger
1 cup corn chips, crushed
1 egg
1 tablespoon chili powder
1 teaspoon ground cumin
¹/₂ teaspoon salt*

1. Combine all ingredients in a
   large bowl and mix until well
   blended.
2. Divide into four balls and shape
   into patties.
3. Grill over medium coals about 4
   to 6 minutes per side until burgers
   are browned and the middle is no
   longer pink.

Makes four servings.

Campfire Corn

*Corn on the cob, with husks
Water
Butter, to taste
Salt, to taste
Herb seasoning, to taste*

1. Pull back the leafy husks of the
   corn just enough to pull out the
   silky strands. Wrap the leaves
   over the ears again and soak the
   corncobs in a large pot of water.
2. Shake the excess water off the
   corncobs and place them on top
   of the edges of hot coals.
3. Allow them to cook for about 15
   minutes, then use tongs to
   remove them from the coals.
4. Test the readiness with a fork:
   when a pricked kernel is soft
   enough to eat, allow the corn to
   cool, then peel back the husks,
   and eat plain, or rub with a little
   butter, herbs, or salt to taste.

Roasted Apple Pockets

Apples, whole
2 tablespoons raisins per apple
1 teaspoon brown sugar per apple
$1/2$ teaspoon cinnamon per apple
Aluminum foil

1. With a paring knife, core each apple, but save a bit of the top with the stem intact, jack-o'-lantern-style.
2. Fill the center with raisins, brown sugar, and cinnamon, then replace the apple's top.
3. Wrap each apple in aluminum foil and set atop the dying embers for about 15 minutes.
3. Remove the apple with tongs, and when foil has cooled enough to touch, bite into the gooey hot apple, or enjoy with a spoon.

LEGENDARY TALL TALES: WILD BILL HICKOCK & CALAMITY JANE

two of the wildest, craziest, toughest characters in the Old West were Wild Bill Hickock and Calamity Jane. The fantastic tales told about them could fill an encyclopedia, and what makes them even more amazing is that this pair actually existed!

Wild Bill's real name was James Butler Hickock. He got his nickname from his wild antics and daring feats. Even as a young boy, people knew his life would be full of adventure. As a teenager, he became an expert marksman with a gun and held a number of strange and wonderful jobs. He was a canal driver, a scout, and even a spy for the Union Army during the Civil War.

Wild Bill hated wearing his stiff Sunday clothes as a child, and disliked it even more when he was a young man. Oftentimes he would wear his clothes over and over again until they were filthy and people could smell him coming from a mile away.

One night, Wild Bill was driving a stagecoach across the frontier. It was getting late, so he decided to settle down and sleep beneath the stars. No sooner had he drifted off to sleep then he heard a strange snuffling sound coming from nearby. He cracked open his eyes. . . and saw a huge brown bear only five feet away from him!

Apparently, Wild Bill's clothing had smelled so strongly of bacon grease and other foods he had spilt on it that the bear had sniffed him out. Wild Bill lay absolutely still and watched the bear paw through his campground. He knew his guns were too far away to reach, and it was only a matter of time before the bear found him. The only thing he had to protect himself was his trusty knife. Quick as a flash, Wild Bill jumped up and ran at the bear. Even though it was surprised, the bear was ready for a fight. The ferocious bear clawed and bit Wild Bill again and again. Even with its razor-sharp claws and immense strength, the bear had met its match in Wild Bill. The battle was long and hard, but finally Wild Bill overcame the mighty bear using only his wits and his knife. After the battle, he struggled home to nurse his many wounds. Amazed people couldn't believe this wild story, and his reputation only grew bigger.

His strange adventures didn't end there. Even though Wild Bill loved to raise a ruckus and was known to be a big-time gambler, he was named U.S. Marshal of several rough Western towns. He was involved in many shoot-outs and single-handedly bested the McCanles gang—

which contained more than ten men! He even grew his hair long as a challenge to the hostile Native Americans who scalped people they fought on the frontier. It seemed like there was no one who cast a bigger shadow in the American West than Wild Bill Hickock . . . until he came to Deadwood, South Dakota and met Calamity Jane.

Calamity Jane was born Martha Jane Cannary, and she was raised in an army camp. Being orphaned at a young age, she learned how to take care of herself and shoot, fight, and ride a horse as well as the best cowboy. Not many jobs were available to women, but that didn't stop Calamity Jane from trying her hand at a number of occupations, most times dressing herself like a boy. She was even a Pony Express rider and braved the treacherous trails to bring messages from town to town. On one occasion, she saved a stagecoach that was being attacked by Native Americans by taking control of the horses when the driver was injured.

When Wild Bill Hickock and Calamity Jane got together in Deadwood, they raised enough noise to wake the dead! Deadwood was a notoriously rough town, but Wild Bill and Calamity Jane were surely the wildest of any of the cowboys. If they weren't racing through town on swift horses, they were whooping it up in the local saloons, or having a grand time at one of their many card games. They competed against each other over any little bet, and were constantly daring each other to do more outrageous and dangerous acts. The two were quite a pair, and some even thought they had been secretly married, although this was never proven.

Wild Bill Hickock later joined up with Buffalo Bill's Wild West Show as an expert shooter. He visited the whole country and met many different people. Unfortunately, he also got into many fights. It was because of one such fight that he was tragically killed. When Calamity Jane heard the news about her dear friend, she vowed to avenge his death, but she never found his killer.

Even though she missed Wild Bill, Calamity Jane was still as wild as ever. She was always full of surprises, and one of her greatest was when she began caring for smallpox victims. Smallpox was a terrible, deadly disease at the time, and many people were amazed that Calamity, who could be so wild and fierce, could also be gentle and loving with her patients. When she passed away, she asked to be buried next to her good friend, Wild Bill. To this day there are no two people who represented the ways of the Wild West better than Calamity Jane and Wild Bill Hickock.

The Old Dame & Her Maids

In olden times, before there were alarm clocks, an old lady kept a rooster in her yard, which would crow at dawn and wake her up each morning. The old lady then got up and woke her maids so that they could begin the day's work. The maids didn't like waking up so early in the morning, so one day they stole the rooster and left it far away from the house.

The next day, the old lady slept until very late because she did not hear the rooster crow. When she found out that the maids had driven the rooster away and she had no way of telling time, she woke the maids up ten times every night because she was afraid they would all oversleep. So instead of sleeping later, the maids got very little sleep!

Moral: What seems like the easy answer to a problem sometimes makes the problem worse.

Everything comes to him who hustles while he waits.
—THOMAS EDISON

Never give in, never give in, never, never, never, never—in nothing great or small, large or petty— never give in except to convictions of honor and good sense.
—WINSTON CHURCHILL

A journey of a thousand miles begins with a single step.
—LAO-TZU

Everyone has inside of him a piece of good news. The good news is that you don't know how great you can be!
—ANNE FRANK

The greatest accomplishment is not in never falling,
but in rising again after you fall.
—VINCE LOMBARDI

■

If at first you don't succeed, try, try, try again.
—W. E. HICKSON

■

You may encounter many
defeats, but you must not
be defeated.
—MAYA ANGELOU

■

When you get to the
end of your rope, tie a
knot and hang on.
—FRANKLIN D. ROOSEVELT

Roadside Lemonade Stand

*M*ost of us remember the thrill we had the very first time we earned pocket money. As any successful entrepreneur knows, the secret to earning your own hard, cold cash lies in seeking out opportunities that fulfill a need in the community. On a hot summer day, you can count on people getting thirsty—meaning that, if you have a roadside lemonade stand, chances are very good that people will stop to drink. Here are some tried-and-true lemonade-stand secrets that you and your grandchildren can use to increase business and add more coins to the piggy bank.

MAKE A STAND

The more professional your operation looks, the more likely people will be to stop and taste your wares. Setting up a table, booth, or stand with an umbrella will attract more customers than simply sitting in a lawn chair next to a cooler. Try these simple ideas:

- Stack a wooden plank or old bookshelf on top of milk crates or cinder blocks. Cover with a decorative picnic-style tablecloth, or paint, stencil, or decorate the plank. Shelves make perfect areas for cups, napkins, a cooler, and your cash box.

- Create a canopy for a small wooden table. You'll need four $3\frac{1}{2}$- to 4-foot-long laths or similar wood strips (which can be purchased at a hardware store), a drill, some screws, tacks, strong flexible wire, and enough fabric to drape over the frame. Fasten a lath firmly to each table leg with two screws so that it sticks up above the table and doesn't rotate. Place a tack in the top of each lath and stretch the wire around the tacks to connect the four poles. Drape the fabric over the frame and use additional tacks to secure it in place.

ADVERTISE

Let people know where you are and what you're selling.

- Use colorful sidewalk chalk to draw arrows several blocks away in every direction and point people your way.
- Make signs on poster board that you can attach to nearby telephone poles or lampposts.
- Make a sandwich board advertising your location and have your partner wear it at a corner of a busy intersection.

PICK YOUR SPOT

Location can be everything. Think ahead to make your lemonade spot work for you.

- Set up your stand where there will be heavy pedestrian traffic.
- If there are bicyclists in your area, avoid being on a significant slope—peddlers may not want to stop in the middle of an uphill climb or downhill coast.
- Put your stand near a shady tree or grassy area to encourage folks to sip in the shade and cool off.

QUALITY QUENCHERS

The first drink might be easy to sell, but you'll get repeat customers with fresh ingredients.

- Set a bowl of fresh lemons, limes, and oranges on your stand. It'll let people know they're getting real juice.
- Don't dilute. Keep a separate cooler for ice and wait until you get an order before pouring lemonade over ice.
- Offer a variety. Keep bottles of club soda or seltzer on hand to make lemonade spritzers. For some failsafe recipes, try Old-time Quenchers, page 72.

Do your ears hang low?
Do they wobble to and fro'?
Can you tie them in a knot?
Can you tie them in a bow?
Can you throw them over your shoulder
  like a Continental soldier?
Do your ears hang low?

Do your ears hang high?
Do they reach up to the sky?
Do they droop when they're wet?
Do they stiffen when they're dry?
Can you semaphore your neighbor
  with a minimum of labor?
Do your ears hang high?

Do your ears hang wide?
Do they flap from side to side?
Do they wave in the breeze?
From the slightest little sneeze?
Can you soar above the nation with
   a feeling of elation?
Do your ears hang wide?

Do your ears fall off?
When you give a great big cough?
Do they lie there on the ground?
Or bounce up at every sound?
Can you stick them in your pocket
   just like little Davy Crockett?
Do your ears fall off?

Do Your Ears Hang Low?

I've often thought

I've often thought
how nice 'twould be
To gallop through
the sky,

To glide o'er towns
and churches,
And pass the steam
cars by.

But when my horse
begins to "break"
And go to pieces
too,

I've often thought
it would be hard
To see just what
to do.

The Child & The Brook

An old man who saw a child stand for a long time by the side of a stream, said, "My child, why do you gaze so long on this brook?" "Sir," said the child, "I stay here to wait until the stream has dried up, for then I can pass with dry feet." "No." The old man chuckled. "You might wait here your entire life and yet not do that, for this brook will run on as long as time. And as you grow up, you will find this out. Either follow the stream to get to sea or get your feet wet!"

Moral: It's better to be active than to wait for things to happen.

Peanut Pals

Peanuts are a delicious and healthy snack you can find in almost any household. These clever little peanut toys are sure to put a smile on your grandchild's face! Peanut-shell finger buddies are a snap to create and can be decorated a million different ways. And peanut pets are adorable mini-friends that can keep kids busy for an entire afternoon. Try putting on a peanut puppet show or peanut circus!

PEANUT FINGER BUDDIES

Shell some large peanuts by breaking the shells in half crosswise. Put an empty half-shell on the tip of a finger and draw a face on it with crayons or markers. Cover all fingers with peanut-shell faces, and have them talk to each other. It's a peanut-buddy party! You can even sew on hats or hair using a large needle and thread and bits of fabric, ribbon, or yarn. Or leave a peanut whole and draw a face on the shell. Then make a stand for the peanut by joining the ends of a strip of paper to make a ring that is slightly smaller than the peanut. Prop up the nut inside.

PEANUT PETS

■ Make a charming peanut puppy from a whole peanut in the shell by making two small holes at each end of the shell and inserting four matchsticks for legs. Add a short matchstick for a tail. Decorate the shell by drawing on a nose, eyes, and mouth with markers, and glue on two ears made from tiny pieces of paper. Or create a lovable lion. For the mane, cut a circle out of fabric, fringe the outer edge with scissors, and cut a small hole in the middle for the peanut to fit through. Alternatively, simply fringe the edge of a strip of paper and join the ends to make a ring. For the tail, color a small bit of cotton from a cotton ball yellow, and glue it to the end of the matchstick tail.

■ A peanut in the shell is also the perfect shape for making a cuddly little bunny. Prop a large peanut up on one end, draw eyes, nose, mouth, and whiskers with marker or crayon, and glue on two long ears made from paper. Don't forget to glue some cotton from a cotton ball to his back to make his tail!

■ Create a wise old owl by standing a peanut up on its large end and propping it in a stand or a little bit of modeling clay. Draw on a face using markers or crayons, and glue on ears and wings made of bits of feathers or shredded paper.

How Many Seconds?

BY CHRISTINA ROSSETTI

How many seconds in a minute?
Sixty, and no more in it.

How many minutes in an hour?
Sixty for sun and shower.

How many hours in a day?
Twenty-four for work and play.

How many days in a week?
Seven both to hear and speak.

How many weeks in a month?
Four, as the swift moon runn'th.

How many months in a year?
Twelve the almanack makes clear.

How many years in an age?
One hundred says the sage.

How many ages in time?
No one knows the rhyme.

As I was walking down the street,
Down the street, down the street,
A pretty girl I chanced to meet
Under the silv'ry moon.

Chorus
Buffalo gals, won't you come out tonight
Come out tonight, come out tonight.
Buffalo gals, won't you come out tonight
And dance by the light of the moon.

I asked her if she'd stop and talk,
Stop and talk, stop and talk.
Her feet took up the whole sidewalk;
She was fair to view.

Chorus

I asked her if she'd be my wife,
Be my wife, be my wife.
Then I'd be happy all my life
If she'd marry me.

Chorus

Buffalo
Gals

Undercover Book Vault

Never judge a book by its cover, the old adage goes. That couldn't be truer than with this crafty project, which turns an old hardcover into a secret storage box. Pick out the perfect hardcover book for a vault with your grandchildren. Younger grandchildren will delight in watching the transformation. Older grandchildren can help measure and glue the box frame.

Large, sturdy hardcover book at least 2" in thickness (the bigger and stronger, the better), measuring tape or ruler, pencil, scissors, X-acto knife, cardboard, glue

1. Open the book you plan to transform and turn a few pages past the title page. (These are the pages that you'll leave in the book.) The right-hand page is the one that you will cut. Using a ruler and pencil, draw a rectangle on that page. Leave a border of about 1 inch from the drawn line to each edge of the page.

2. Measure the rectangle that you drew. Then measure the thickness of the book's interior pages. These dimensions will make up the volume of your book vault.

3. Measure and cut four pieces of cardboard to create a frame that matches the dimensions of your book vault.

4. Using an X-acto knife, carefully cut out the interior rectangle of all the pages in the book (except for those first few pages). Be sure to leave the outer borders of the interior pages intact, so it still appears to be a regular book when closed.

5. Glue the last page of the book to the inside of the back cover of the book.

6. Set the cardboard frame along the interior edges of your book vault and glue the frame to the cut edges of the interior pages. Let dry.

7. Now your grandchildren will have a secret compartment in which to store pencils, pens, and trinkets.

Big Little Boy

BY EVE MERRIAM

"Me oh my," said the tiny, shiny ant,
"I can crawl all the way up a sand hill,
A hill so high it's as big as a thimble.
Can any creature in the world be bigger than I?"

"Skat," said the green caterpillar,
"I can inch myself all the way across a twig.
Now a twig is really big!
Hooray for great, glorious, mammoth,
 and modest me."

"Gog and magog," said the speckled frog,
"And bilge water. Little ant, crawly caterpillar,
You can only creep.
I can leap!
All the way up to a tremendous lily pad in the pond.
How superiffic can any creature be?
I'll tell you—
He can be me!"

192

"Oh," laughed the little boy,
"Gangway, skedaddle, vamoose.
Look at me, tiny ant. My finger is bigger than a thimble.
Look, inchy caterpillar. My foot is bigger than a twig.
Look, speckled frog. My hand can cover a lily pad all over.
Why, I'm so big I can run in circles, I can run in squares,

I can reach to tables, I can fill up chairs!
And I'm still growing!
When I grow all the way up, my head will bump the sky.
I'll have clouds for a bed, and a moon pillow,
And stars instead of freckles on my nose."

(Is that how big a little boy grows?)

Legendary Tall Tales: The Lost Treasure of Captain Kidd

Captain William Kidd was not having a good day. He was all set to leave Great Britain and sail back home to the American colonies. He had been transporting goods between the two continents for many months, and now he couldn't wait to get back and see his family. But just as he was getting ready to head off, two British soldiers stopped him and asked for a word with him. Then they made him an offer he couldn't refuse.

"William Kidd, how would you like to help out your mother country?" one asked.

"Depends on what you're asking," Kidd grumbled.

During the 1600s, pirates plagued the waters between the colonies and Great Britain. These bands of cutthroats stole riches and goods, slaughtered people, and forced others to join their murderous gangs.

The British government requested Captain Kidd become a pirate hunter. His job would be to sail up and down the eastern coast of America, attacking any pirate ship he saw.

Captain Kidd was not happy with this request. After all, he was only a simple sea captain and was eager to see his family again. But you couldn't just say no to the British king, and so Captain Kidd found himself reluctantly searching for pirates.

His crew wasn't very happy with the way things worked out either. "Why do we have to search for these bloody pirates?" his first mate, Smith asked.

"King's orders. Gotta do what the king says," Kidd answered.

"But we've been sailing for ages, and we haven't seen a single pirate ship."

The rest of the crew agreed, and Kidd

was afraid there would be a mutiny soon.

As the sun dipped below the horizon, they suddenly spotted a large ship in the distance. Kidd and his crew couldn't quite make out the flag, but everyone agreed that it looked like a pirate ship loaded with bounty. He reluctantly told the crew to open fire on the mysterious ship, and they soon captured it. But imagine their dismay when they realized that the ship was actually a member of the English fleet! Instead of protecting his country from pirates, Captain Kidd had accidentally become one!

He knew he'd be wanted for piracy if he returned to England, and that he'd be arrested immediately if he set foot in America. The only place left for him to go was Madagascar, a notorious pirate haven.

Captain Kidd knew he was in a terrible bind, but he didn't know what else to do. His crew convinced him that they might as well continue with their piracy, since they were already wanted men. And

he was still angry with the British government for putting him in this situation.

"I could've been home with my loving wife, curled up by the fire, enjoying a cup of chowder, and instead I'm out wandering the oceans, no better then a common cutthroat!" he told himself. And from that day forward, he and his crew captured many treasure-laden ships.

For a person who had begun his career as a law-abiding sea captain, Captain Kidd became quite the pirate. Within a few years his riches piled up, and his name was one of the most feared in the world. But money and riches didn't matter to him if he couldn't be with his family. He finally decided to sail for America and reunite with them.

The ship pulled along the coast of New Jersey, and Captain Kidd made his preparations to go ashore.

"Now, crew," he advised them, "I'm done with this life of piracy. We'll divide up the booty, and each man can go his own way. Agreed?" The crew gave their oaths, and the fabulous wealth was divvied up. Captain Kidd himself had two huge chests full of gold and jewels, which he buried in a secret location. Once he found his family, he would come back and reclaim his riches.

But this was not to be. When Captain Kidd arrived at his house, he found it empty. Although he knew he was a wanted man, he frantically ran to his neighbor's house to find out what happened. Imagine that man's surprise when he found the notorious Captain Kidd standing on his doorstep!

"No one knows what happened to your family, William," the man managed to gasp. "They didn't hear from you for so long that they thought you had died. One day, your wife and children packed up and left."

Captain Kidd was heartbroken and continued to search madly for his family, but no one knew where they had gone. Completely alone and miserable, he decided to give himself up to the local constables.

"After all, all the gold in the world is nothing if I don't have my family." He sighed.

Captain Kidd was arrested and sentenced to be executed. To this day, some people say you can still see his ghostly ship floating off the coast of Long Island and Cape May, New Jersey, still searching for the family he left long ago.

As for the fantastic riches he buried, no one has ever found them. Thousands of treasure hunters have searched for the booty over the years. To this day the legendary treasure of Captain Kidd remains safely hidden, perhaps waiting for its ghostly owner to return and claim it once again.

Refrigerator Cakes

There's something sweet and delectable about taking an afternoon to bake a traditional cake using old-fashioned ingredients just like your grandparents used to. Nevertheless, making homemade cakes and pies doesn't have to take all day: There's always a secret shortcut for something delicious. Making the best cakes doesn't require an oven—the refrigerator will do just fine. These desserts are simple to make and are yummy with a glass of milk.

Pineapple Crunch Cake

1 ($1/4$-ounce) package plain gelatin
$1/2$ cup confectioners' sugar
$1/4$ cup butter, room temperature
1 egg yolk, beaten
$1/2$ cup crushed pineapple
$1/4$ cup chopped walnuts
1 egg white, whipped until stiff
18 graham crackers
Whipped cream as garnish

1. Prepare gelatin using package directions and set aside to cool.
2. In large bowl, mix sugar, butter, and beaten egg yolk together. Stir in pineapple and walnuts and blend well. Fold in egg white.

3. In a 9- by 11-inch baking dish spread a layer of graham crackers so they fit snugly along the bottom.
4. Top with filling and chill 4 hours in refrigerator until cake is set.
5. Serve with a dollop of cream.

Makes six to eight servings.

Strawberry Orange Cake

1 (12-ounce) package ladyfingers
4 cups fresh orange juice
$1 1/2$ cups sugar
3 ($1/4$-ounce) packages plain gelatin
$1/3$ cup fresh-squeezed lemon juice
$1/8$ teaspoon salt
1 cup heavy whipping cream

198

1 cup diced orange segments
2 cups fresh strawberries, sliced

1. Split ladyfingers in half and layer them on the bottom of an 8-inch springform pan.
2. In small saucepan, stir 1 cup orange juice and sugar over medium heat until sugar dissolves. Remove from heat.
3. In separate bowl, dissolve gelatin in 1 cup orange juice. Stir into hot juice. Add remaining orange juice, lemon juice, and salt to hot juice and stir. Chill until mixture thickens slightly.
4. Whip cream until stiff and fold in to juice mixture. Fold in orange segments.
5. Spoon mixture over ladyfingers and chill for about 4 hours.
6. Arrange sliced strawberries in decorative circular pattern on top.
7. Remove springform sides and place cake on serving platter.

Makes six to eight servings.

Chocolate Cake

2 cups heavy whipping cream
1/4 cup chocolate syrup
1 package chocolate graham crackers or chocolate wafers

1. Chill bowl and beaters in freezer for 1/2 hour.
2. In chilled bowl, whip cream until stiff peaks form. Slowly beat in chocolate syrup.
3. Layer bottom of 12- by 8-inch glass pan with graham crackers or wafers. Add 1/2-inch layer of chocolate cream. Repeat layering with cookies and cream until pan is full.
4. Chill 4 hours in refrigerator before cutting into squares and serving.

Makes about twelve servings.

Ship Ahoy!

Summer is the ideal time to spend at the lake launching new boats in the water and seeing how they sail. Balsa wood, found at your local craft or hardware store, is perfect for such carving projects. Younger grandchildren can enjoy helping with the boat plans while Granddad does the carving. Older grandchildren can hone their woodworking skills and enjoy watching their handiwork float along the shore.

Carving knife; 7"x 1$\frac{1}{2}$" x 2" balsa wood block (for the hull); ruler; drill with $\frac{3}{16}$" bit; sandpaper; waterproof paint; superglue; 5$\frac{1}{2}$ x 6$\frac{1}{2}$" x 6$\frac{1}{2}$" triangle of water-resistant nylon cloth (sail); $\frac{3}{16}$" diameter wooden dowel, 7$\frac{1}{4}$" long (mast); hammer (optional); nail (optional); silicone spray sealant

1. Using the carving knife, cut off 2 corners on the 2-inch side of the 7-inch block of balsa, so that it now looks like one side is pointed. This is the front of the boat, or "bow."

2. About 4 inches from the rear of the boat (or "stern,") drill a hole $\frac{1}{4}$ inch deep for the mast.

3. Sand and paint the boat and allow to dry completely.

4. Glue the shorter side of the sail's triangle onto the mast. Insert a few drops of glue into the hole in the hull and insert the mast. Or attach the mast by hammering a short nail through the bottom of the boat up into the dowel.

5. Spray the finished boat with sealant, and allow to dry before setting sail.

From this valley they say you are going,
We will miss your bright eyes and sweet smile,
For they say you are taking the sunshine,
That brightens our pathway awhile.

Chorus
Come and sit by my side if you love me,
Do not hasten to bid me adieu,
But remember the Red River Valley,
And the girl that has loved you so true.

202

Red River Valley

Won't you think of the valley you're leaving?
Oh, how lonely, how sad it will be,
Oh think of the fond heart you're breaking,
And the grief you are causing me.

Chorus

From this valley they say you are going,
When you go, may your darling go, too?
Would you leave her behind unprotected
When she loves no other but you?

Chorus

I have promised you, darling, that never
Will a word from my lips cause you pain;
And my life, it will be yours forever
If you only will love me again.

There was an Old Man with a Beard

BY EDWARD LEAR

There was an Old Man with a beard,
Who said, "It is just as I feared!—
Two Owls and a Hen, four Larks and a Wren,
Have all built their nests in my beard!"

There was an Old Man of Dumbree

BY EDWARD LEAR

There was an Old Man of Dumbree,
who taught little Owls to drink Tea;
For he said,
"To eat mice is not proper or nice,"
That amiable Man of Dumbree.

206

Ocean Tide-Pooling

Spending a day at the beach can open a world of discovery for young explorers. Low tide reveals the otherwise hidden homes of anemones, hermit crabs, and other sea creatures. When you take your grandchildren trolling along rocky coastlines, see how many different life forms you can identify. In bigger tide-pool areas, you can make your own undersea dredge for seeing things up close. Encourage your grandchildren to tread lightly on fragile coastal areas: What may look like dried up seaweed could rally back to life when the tide rolls in again.

DRYING RACK

24- x 24-inch wooden board or shallow wooden crate (such as a fruit crate from the grocery), tacks

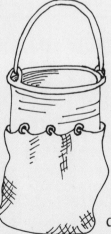

A day tide-pooling might yield an interesting assortment of kelp, sea squirts, hermit crabs, or starfish. The best way to preserve your collection is to spread it on a flat surface in the sun until completely dried out. Use tacks to pin starfish into shape or spread out seaweed.

SEASHORE DREDGE

Small plastic pail with handle, fine-mesh sack (such as onion or potato sacking from the grocery), twine, box cutter or knife, rope

Grandchildren can use a simple dredge along the edges of tide pools or along the ocean floor and get an up-close look at sea life. Cut the bottom out of a plastic bucket and punch several holes around the middle to attach the sack. Through the holes, fasten the sack to the bucket with twine. Tie a line of rope to the handle for dredging off piers or in deep tide pool areas.

Seashore Scenery

■ **LIMPETS** are conical shells commonly found clinging to tidal rocks and seaweeds. They vary in color and often have iridescent interiors.

■ **ROCK SHELLS** and **WHELKS** are the homes of carnivorous snails, commonly found among rocks or pebbly areas at low tide.

■ **SEA ANEMONES** inhabit tide pools, where they attach themselves to the base of rocks or use their tentacles to anchor themselves in the sand.

■ **STARFISH** can often be found in lower tide pools or along open rocky shores, where they feed on shellfish and barnacles.

■ Abundant along high-tide rocks, **BARNACLES** may look like dead crusty formations, but look for their feeding movements under water at high tide.

■ **HERMIT CRABS** like to burrow into muddy coastal flats or upper tide-pool regions.

A Fairy Tale Verse

Rip was a chap who relished fun,
And so when out with dog and gun
He came upon some little men
Who played at nine pins in a glen,
He joined them, drinking deep until
He slumbered, having had his fill.
When he awoke, his beard was gray;
His trusty dog had gone away;

Rip Van Winkle

Changed was the house he'd thought his own,
His children, men and women grown;
And he could scarce believe his ears
To learn he'd slept for twenty years.

Legendary Tall Tales: Daniel Boone and the Great Outdoors

One of the great outdoorsman of America was a man named Daniel Boone. Daniel was born in Pennsylvania around 1734. Some say he had ten brothers and sisters! With that many children running around the house, was it any wonder he spent a lot of his time in the great outdoors? He learned how to hunt and gather and survive off the land at a young age. Never one to back down from a challenge, he was always fascinated by stories of adventures from the unexplored areas of America.

When he got a little older, he met an experienced scout named John Finley. Finley loved to tell stories, especially about a wondrous land over the Appalachian Mountains called Kentucky.

"Why, the hills roll on forever," he told the young Daniel Boone, "There's plenty of space for a man to spread out!"

Daniel considered his crowded household and knew that Kentucky was just the place for him. But he also knew that it would take every ounce of his strength and courage to tame that rugged land. Daniel prepared for this challenge by sharpening his tracking and hunting skills all the way from Pennsylvania to North Carolina. When he finally decided he was ready to tackle Kentucky, he joined a party of five men, including his old friend John Finley. They set off west through the Cumberland Gap, a notoriously treacherous path with steep cliffs.

The tough journey stretched on for days and days, but they finally made it to the beautiful, fertile land of Kentucky.

Daniel loved Kentucky so much that he moved his family there and carved out a path called Wilderness Trail so it would be easier for others to settle.

Daniel Boone continued to explore uncharted areas and used his fantastic outdoor skills to carve a niche out of the rugged landscape. Pioneers said Daniel was such a good tracker and scout that he had the eyes of an eagle and a memory as long as a river.

One time, Daniel found a beautiful area in a forest where the fish practically leaped onto your fishhook, and the leaves turned as bright as gold in the sun. He cut three notches into a young oak tree sapling nearby to mark the spot so he could return to it later on.

Twenty years later, Daniel remembered this special spot and told his friends about it.

"Daniel, that was over two decades ago." They all laughed. "You think you can find this place again because of some little scratches on a tree trunk?"

"I don't *think* I can, I *know* I can!" Daniel declared, and they organized a party to search for it. The group followed Daniel through the wild areas until finally he came to a stop beneath a tall group of trees.

"This is definitely the place," Daniel told them. His friends checked the trees and then began to laugh.

"Daniel, you fool," one said, "there's no marked tree here!"

Daniel Boone studied one of the trees carefully, and then took his knife out and gently scraped off a bit of moss that had grown on the trunk. There, plain as day, were the three marks Daniel had cut into the trunk those many years ago. Daniel Boone had done it, and no one doubted his tracking skills ever again.

Gone Fishin'

The cooler's packed, the tackle box is full, and the fish are biting. What better way to spend a summer day than with your grandchildren on the lake, by the river, or at the ocean? With a little bit of bait and plenty of patience, even novice anglers can bring home the catch of the day. Even if you won't be having trout for dinner, a day spent fishing can be the most enjoyable way to do nothing at all. For beginners and seasoned salts alike, here are some tried and true methods to get more bites and keep the grandkids casting.

HOW TO GET HOOKED

- **STILL FISHING** is the basic "sit and wait" method, off a dock, pier, or rock. Putting weights, or "sinkers," on your line will help you catch fish that swim near the bottom; putting floats or "bobbers" on your line makes it easier to hook fish near the surface.
- There are times when a moving lure, such as a wobbling spoon or spinner bait, will coax a fish into striking. With this type of fishing, called **CASTING**, you continually throw out and reel in your line.
- A combination of still fishing and casting, **TROLLING** is simply dragging a lure and/or live bait off the back of a moving boat and waiting for the fish to bite.
- **FLY-FISHING** is the best way to catch fish that like to eat insects that hover near the water's surface, such as dragonflies. This type of fishing requires special lightweight lures, lines, rods, and reels. Instead of using bait, you tempt the fish with artificial flies, which are beautiful lifelike models made of fur, thread, feathers, and similar materials tied to a hook.

WHEN THE FISH AREN'T BITING

- *Try a different method.* If you've got a sinker on your line, switch to a bobber. If that doesn't work, try a spinner and cast for a while.
- *Move to a new spot.* You know the fish are in the lake, and sometimes you need to find them before they can find you.
- *Switch to a different kind of bait.* Try fish eggs instead of worms or grubs. If you're casting, try a different-colored lure. Try replacing your bait with a spinner.
- *Keep your eyes on other anglers who are reeling in fish.* What are they doing differently? Don't be shy about asking questions—but don't do this in the middle of the lake, as talking loudly will scare away fish! Most fishermen enjoy sharing their love for the sport. See if you can learn from their success.
- *Get your mind off fishing!* Read a book, see if you can spot other wildlife with binoculars, share stories (quietly) with your fishing partner, or play a card game.

Oftentimes, as soon as you forget about the fish, they'll come a-nibblin'.

On top of old Smoky,
All cover'd with snow,
I lost my true lover,
Come a-courtin' too slow.

A-courtin's a pleasure,
A-flirtin's a grief,
A false-hearted lover,
Is worse than a thief.

For a thief, he will rob you,
And take what you have,
But a false-hearted lover
Will send you to your grave.

She'll hug you and kiss you
And tell you more lies
Than the cross-ties on the railroad,
Or the stars in the skies.

On top of old Smoky,
All covered with snow,
I lost my true lover,
A-courtin' too slow.

On Top of Old Smoky

from Ode to Immortality

BY WILLIAM WORDSWORTH

What though the radiance which was once so bright
Be now for ever taken from my sight,
Though nothing can bring back the hour
Of splendor in the grass, of glory in the flower,
We will grieve not, rather find
Strength in what remains behind;

Star Sense

*T*he nighttime can be frightening for young children, especially when darkness and shadows conceal the world as they know it in the daytime. But with some special tips on how to use the stars to their advantage, children can not only overcome nervousness about the dark, but actually look forward to using their newfound nocturnal abilities. On the next clear, starry night you spend with your grandchildren, share these fun secrets about the stars and see how they improve their star sense.

KNOW HOW FAR NORTH YOU ARE

*O*n a clear night, you can show your grandchildren the same star by which mariners have navigated since ancient times. Polaris, also called the Pole Star or the North Star, is easy to spot once you locate the Big Dipper. If you follow a line through the outer two stars of the Big Dipper's "ladle" (Merak and Dubhe), it will point to Polaris, the first star in the "handle" of the Little Dipper.

Once your grandchildren locate Polaris, they can use a hand as a measuring device to determine how far north of the equator they're standing. When you hold your hand

20°

at arm's length in front of you, each finger covers about two degrees. If you spread your fingers wide, pinky tip to thumb tip covers about twenty degrees. Using your hand, measure the degrees between the horizon and the North Star. There are 69 miles in a degree. So, to calculate the number of miles north of the equator you're standing, simply multiply the number of degrees by 69.

LISTEN TO A FALLING STAR

Stargazing is always fun during meteor showers when you can spend the night counting falling stars. But what if there's cloud cover? No problem—there's more than one way to catch a falling star. Just tune in to an FM radio and instead of watching meteors fall, you and your grandchildren can listen to them. A meteor leaves a trail of ions as it falls. These particles register as *pings* that sound like a tone, a bit of music, or static on FM stations. With an FM/TV antenna, you can best catch these *pings* on a radio tuned between 88 and 108 MHz.

IMPROVE YOUR NIGHT VISION

You and your grandchildren may not have night vision goggles or the keen eyesight of a nocturnal critter, but you can still learn how to see better in the dark. The secret is to use an old astronomer's trick called "averted vision." On a clear night when you can see the stars, simply look off to one side of the object that you're viewing. After doing this for a while, you'll notice that the object will appear brighter than when looking at it directly. Explain to your grandchildren the reason for this has to do with the design of our eyes. When we look at something directly, we are using the iris, made of cone cells, which allow us to see better in bright light.

When we look at something off-center, we're taking advantage of our rod cells, which allow us to see better in the dark.

Another way to see the stars better at night is by using a sighting tube. Any long, cylindrical tube, such as a cardboard tube for a poster or wrapping paper, can become a sighting tube. Simply cup one eye with your hand and peer into the sky through the tube with the other eye. The sighting tube will cut down on nearby light pollution from streetlights or a campfire and can make dim stars appear brighter.

Leisure

BY WILLIAM HENRY DAVIES

What is life if, full of care,
We have no time to stand and stare.

No time to stand beneath the boughs
And stare as long as sheep or cows.

No time to see, when woods we pass,
Where squirrels hide their nuts in grass.

No time to see, in broad daylight,
Streams full of stars, like stars at night.

No time to turn at Beauty's glance,
And watch her feet, how they can dance.

No time to wait till her mouth can
Enrich that smile her eyes began.

A poor life this if, full of care,
We have no time to stand and stare.

I've often thought

How nice the big
new moon would be
For little me to
sit in.
'Twould be a cozy
rocking chair
That sleepy me
would fit in.

HOW TO
TAME
WILD
FLOWER

But if the moon
got very full
And just a little
frisky.
Perhaps my cozy
rocking chair
Would be a little
risky.